Backroading
Vancouver
Island

Backroading
Vancouver
Island

Rosemary Neering

Whitecap Books
Vancouver / Toronto

The information in this book is true and complete to the best of our knowledge. All recommendations are made without guarantee on the part of the author or Whitecap Books Ltd. The author and publisher disclaim any liability in connection with the use of this information. For additional information please contact Whitecap Books Ltd., 351 Lynn Avenue, North Vancouver, BC, V7J 2C4.

Edited by Elaine Jones
Cover design by DesignGeist
Cover photo by Paul Price
Interior design by Warren Clark
Typeset by Warren Clark

Printed and bound in Canada.

Canadian Cataloguing in Publication Data

Neering, Rosemary, 1945–
    Backroading Vancouver Island

    Includes index.
    ISBN 1-55110-401-6
    1. Rural roads—British Columbia—Vancouver Island, Guidebooks.
2. Vancouver Island (B.C.)—Guidebooks. I. Title.
FC3844.2.N43 1996   917.11204'4   C95-911143-3
F1089.V3N43 1996

Disclaimer
The author, editor and publisher of *Backroading Vancouver Island* have used their best efforts to inform the reader as to the risks inherent in travelling the routes described in this book. The level of expertise required to travel into largely unmarked, remote and hazardous areas must be decided by the reader. Safety is the responsibility of the individual. We take no responsibility for any loss or injury incurred by anyone using information contained in this book.

Acknowledgements

Thanks are due to all those who read parts of the manuscript and suggested changes or corrections. Among that number are Janis Leach, Ministry of Forests, Campbell River; Bruce McCulloch, Brian Voth, and Mike Dietsch, Western Forests Products on the North Island; Russell Thompson, Cameron Young, and Mark Zuehlke. Thanks also to the many people along the way who suggested back-road routes, provided information about the roads or sites of interest, or pointed me towards research sources.

The phrase "without whose help this book could not have been written" has become a cliché. But sometimes, the cliché is true. This is one of those times. My heartfelt thanks to Joe Thompson who drove these roads with me, putting up with endless cries of, "What was that back there?" and "Oops—can we turn around?" His ability to suss out the land while I was wrestling with upside down and incomplete maps, to ask passersby in pickup trucks for help, to assess roads as passable when I was getting timid, and to make U-turns on roads barely wider than the car was long made much of this book possible.

CONTENTS

Backroading
Vancouver Island

PEOPLE WHO KNOW ME DON'T ASK FOR A RIDE WHEN THEY WANT to get somewhere in a hurry. A simple half-hour Victoria to Sidney excursion is likely to turn into a three-hour odyssey as I pick up bread from a roadside stall on one back road, watch the lambs gambolling in the fields beside another, and photograph daffodils just peeking into flower down on the flats that can't be seen from the highway. I suspect the phrase, "To travel is better than to arrive," was coined for me.

Of course, there are times when schedules must be met and arriving is the point. But for me, true contentment comes when there is no schedule and no set-in-stone destination, and I can wander away from the highway on back roads and country roads. My eyes glaze over when friends boast of making it to Calgary overnight, of driving across the country in forty-eight hours non-stop, or of spending a vacation on the freeway. Where, I always want to ask, is the fun in that?

So don't ask me how long it takes to get from the south end of Vancouver Island to Port Hardy at the north end, a distance by highway of some 500 kilometres. "Four days," I'm likely to tell you, "though you'll miss some of the best back roads if you hurry like that."

As Vancouver Island fills up with more and more newcomers who have discovered its moderate climate and marvellous views, residents call for improvements to the direct routes. The B.C. government publishes advertisements declaring that, by the year 1999, most of the kinks and bottlenecks between Victoria and Campbell River will have been straightened or bypassed, and a traveller will be able to make the 250-kilometre journey in less than three hours.

That will leave the back roads to me and people like me, who would rather wander through the countryside at a sedate pace, discovering the roadside farm stands, the pubs, the forests, the wild flowers, the ocean views, and, yes, the potholes, mud, dust and dead-ends that back roads surprise you with.

Vancouver Island back roads are of two types and two origins. Some were once main roads, following the contours of the land to link settlements along the coast or on rivers and lakes. These early roads replaced or enhanced travel by water and were in turn replaced by straighter, faster highways.

Most of these back roads, almost always paved and suitable for the most timid Sunday driver, lie between the Island Highway and the waters east of the island, or run for short stretches along valleys west of the main highway. By these roadsides are farm stands, farm fields, small towns, pubs and cafes, views over the water, parks to hike in, and coves to linger at.

Other back roads were built for other purposes. Most began life as logging roads, built by forest companies to allow loggers access to timber. A detailed map of Vancouver Island shows it honeycombed with logging roads, which in some areas seem to circle every mountain, ride every ridge, follow every stream. Other roads of this type led to mines high on mountains, to abandoned towns built decades ago by hopeful miners, and to shrinking villages where a handful of people still live despite the closure of mills and mines.

Though some of these roads are paved, most are gravel. They range from wide, fairly straight stretches to steep, winding, narrow, muddy or dusty roads that would make you want to turn around and go back if turning around wasn't more heart-stopping than going on.

Both paved country roads and gravel logging roads appear in this book. We have driven every road that I describe in detail in a stout two-wheel-drive passenger car, despite the anguished moans of my mechanic every time I returned from a trip. Total toll: several mufflers, several brake jobs, and a permanent coat of dust on inaccessible crannies of the car's interior.

To drive these gravel roads, however, you must remain undismayed by the occasional stretch of bone-jarring, muffler-threatening washboard, dust that cakes your car inside and out and does the same to you, road closures that make you retrace your route when you were within a few kilometres of your ultimate destination, and road conditions that can change from week to week.

This isn't a catalogue of back roads on the island. There are too many, and describing them all would be dull and hopelessly repetitious. The trips in this book are my favourites, for a Sunday-afternoon jaunt, an all-day exploration, or a several-day vacation. They are for people who are quite content to spend time getting there, if they ever get around to defining just where "there" might be.

On Driving Logging Roads

A passenger car rarely wins an argument with a five-metre-wide off-road logging truck. Though most of the logging roads mentioned in this book are open all the time, some are not: signs indicate that you can drive them only in the evenings and on weekends. Some drivers like to disregard these signs. "It will be okay, won't it?" one such driver asked me. "They can't really keep me off the roads."

Well, maybe they can and maybe they can't, but when you meet logging traffic on an active logging road, the logging traffic probably can't and undoubtedly won't stop to let you past. These big trucks barrel along, and it's unlikely they'll see you in time to stop, even if they wanted to.

So: obey the basic rules. Watch for signs indicating road closures, because of active logging or forest-fire hazard. Inquire at company offices about industrial traffic on the roads you want to use, and drive with your headlights on at all times, so you are at least a little more visible. Watch for pull-outs as you navigate narrow roads, so you know where you can back up to should you need to pull over to let a truck by.

Listen to the locals. I mean really listen. I asked at a local forest company office if we could drive a particular logging road during a weekday. Given that I had already phoned the forest information centre from Victoria, and been assured the road was open, it seemed a good bet. "I wouldn't," said the woman behind the desk. The road is closed? "No, it's open, but there's a lot of trucks out there this week. We got our truck smashed up out there last week. Logging truck came down the hill and there was nowhere for the driver to go but into the rock. So, I wouldn't go."

"I wouldn't," is localese for, "Do any damn thing you want to, but don't expect us to pick up the pieces. Too many fool tourists around here anyway."

Locals are the only people who know whether a road is being used on any given day, whether a section of road has washed out, whether a bridge is being replaced, whether there is anything of interest along the road.

And they'll be happy to tell you, providing you don't show your colours as a superior city slicker. A grizzled veteran of the back country once decided we were okay, unlike some other visitors he'd talked to a week or so before. "Had a couple of young guys here by the lake a while back. They just stood there and watched me load all my gear in the boat, take three or four trips from the truck, never offered to help. Then when I was finished, they came over and asked me where the fishing was good. 'Well,' I said, 'the water flows in down that end of the lake,' " he pointed up the lake, " 'and goes out the other end, and the fish all go with it. No fish in this lake.' So they jumped in their truck and off they went to the lake downstream." He grinned, then told us—since we had no fishing gear— where the fish really were, said one much-ballyhooed local attraction wasn't worth the gas it took to get there, and mentioned a new old-growth forest trail across the lake.

Collect all the maps you can find of the back roads. No two will agree. If one shows a road to the left, another will show it to the right, and yet another will suggest both are closed because the bridges are out. Logging roads change: new routes are built, old routes are barricaded or washed out by cascading streams, and road status changes from active to inactive or vice versa. In general, the recreation guides and maps published by the forest companies are the most reliable. But even then, you will find roads closed that you thought were open, roads rough where a year ago they were smooth.

In any case, take all the maps along when you tackle a convoluted back-road route. Arguing about which map is right will give you something to do when you get lost.

Be prepared. Basic necessities are a full tank of gas, extra water and oil, a good spare tire (we once drove to Carmanah and back unaware that our spare was completely flat; the gods were on our side that day, but they are capricious), enough food and drink to keep you going if your car does break down or if you have an accident, and a sleeping bag or two, just in case.

Many spur roads lead from the logging roads mentioned in this book. We recommend that you stay off these roads if you are driving a two-wheel-drive vehicle, or if your four-wheel-drive vehicle has low clearance. Though these roads may be passable at first, they often become steep and narrow, have high centres or ruts too wide for a passenger car, are "paved" with large, sharp gravel, or have sections with deep potholes or wash-outs. Because they are narrow, with no shoulders, it is difficult to make a U-turn.

✤ ✤ ✤

We take no responsibility for the continued driveability of roads described in this book. Roads change; the condition of logging roads in particular can change from week to week. You have to use your common sense on any back road, turning back whenever it appears that conditions warrant. Check that your car insurance covers you when you are on logging roads, and be aware British Columbia Automobile Association services do not apply on these roads.

And one further note of warning: many of the trails or hikes mentioned in this book are in isolated areas. When you park your car, lock your valuables in the trunk or take them with you. Locked trunks won't deter determined thieves, but they may deter the casual window-smasher.

Resources

Each chapter contains a list of maps you may find useful on travels in that area. The following resources are more general, or cover more than one area.

Blier, Richard. *Island Adventures* and *More Island Adventures*. Victoria: Orca Book Publishers, 1989 and 1993. Intended mainly for the outdoor recreationist, these books cover many logging road areas throughout the island.

Lillard, Charles. *Seven Shillings a Year*. Ganges: Horsdal and Schubart, 1986. A general history of Vancouver Island.

Merriman, Alec and Taffy. *Logging Road Travel, Vol. 1, Victoria to Campbell River; Vol. 2, Campbell River to Cape Scott.* Sidney: Saltaire Publishing, 1973. Long out of print but still available at second-hand bookstores, these books are the original backroaders' companions. Merriman campaigned long and hard for public access to land where timber rights were leased by logging companies; when he wrote his books, the gates were just opening. Though many of the roads have changed since then and many new ones have been built, these books are still well worth having.

Northern Vancouver Island, Recreation and Relief Map. Vancouver: G.M. Johnson and Associates Ltd., 1994. A reasonably good general map from Courtenay to Port Hardy.

Guide to Forest Land of Southern Vancouver Island. Co-operative project of forest companies and the provincial Ministry of Forests. Logging roads, Victoria to Qualicum and Port Alberni.

CHAPTER 1

The Victoria Region

MANY A VISITOR COMES TO VICTORIA, THEN RETURNS TO THE mainland thinking he has seen Vancouver Island. But the small southern fraction of the island is different from the rest.

It's a difference noted early by nineteenth-century explorers and fur traders, who viewed the island's southern tip with great glee. Instead of the endless forests that they considered gloomy and unwelcoming, the inhospitable coast that offered little harbour for their ships, the looming mountains that denied any chance at farming, they found here pleasant meadows, safe harbour, and wide, rolling land topped with fertile soil.

While much of Vancouver Island other than the narrow east-coast plain receives torrents of rain, the southern tip lies in a rain shadow, and is the year-round warmest, driest part of the island. Hemlock, Sitka spruce, and cedar dominate the forests to the north; here Garry oak, arbutus, and Douglas-fir dominate, and spring wildflowers carpet the meadows.

Climate and geography combined to encourage settlement, and the southern tip of the island is now home to half a million people, more than half of the island's population squeezed into a small portion of its land. Yet, surprisingly, and mostly because the imposition of the Agricultural Land Reserve prevented wholesale development, many a back road remains free of subdivisions and shopping malls, luring the driver into Sunday-afternoon expeditions.

The roads I describe in these tours are the ones that, living in Victoria, I drive most often. Fed up with the city, tired of sitting in front of a computer screen, or just wanting a relaxed drive at any hour of the day, any season of the year, I wander out to the Saanich Peninsula, past moss-covered rocks and arbutus, seeking fresh raspberries or apples or bedding plants, lunch or latte or a beer. Or I head towards Sooke, out along the lagoon and ocean, revelling in pounding waves, gentle coves, long cobble beaches, cutting inland on the occasional gravel logging road. I have probably driven these roads a thousand times; they rarely fail to soothe the spirit.

Resources

General maps of Greater Victoria, the Saanich Peninsula, and the Western Communities, available from most newsstands and stationers, cover the area from Victoria north to Sidney, and Goldstream west to Sooke. Beyond Sooke, try the *Guide to Forest Land of Southern Vancouver Island*, available from the Ministry of Forests, logging company offices, and some tourist infocentres.

Many books exist on the human and natural history of the Victoria region. Among the most helpful:

Chaster, G.D. et al. *Trees of Greater Victoria: A Heritage*. Victoria: Heritage Tree Book Society, 1988.

Grant, Peter. *The Altitude Guide to Victoria*. Altitude Press, 1994.

Weston, Jim, and Stirling, David, ed. *The Naturalist's Guide to the Victoria Region*. Victoria: Victoria Natural History Society, 1986.

Zuehlke, Mark. *The Vancouver Island South Explorer*. Vancouver: Whitecap Books, 1994.

 **THE SAANICH PENINSULA**

Circle tour, approximately 75 kilometres on paved roads around the Saanich Peninsula, starting and ending near Royal Oak, though drivers can choose any point on the tour to begin their wanderings. This tour can take two hours or a full day, depending on how long you linger.

The back roads of the Saanich peninsula are the most used of the roads described in this book. Yet, even though housing spreads ever farther across the Saanich Peninsula, and the back roads are becoming ever busier, they can still be surprisingly restful: for the most part, traffic in a hurry follows the main highway, leaving the back roads that wind through farmland and forest for the more relaxed among us.

These roads are suitable for all cars and drivers, and for bicycles. They meander through Garry oak, arbutus, cedar, and fir; along lakeside and seashore; past farm fields with many farm produce stands in season; through Indian reserve lands. En route are short strolls and longer hikes near roads; old churches and cemeteries; pubs and cafes; marinas, farm markets and stands, museums. All seasons.

Before You Go

Any map of the Saanich Peninsula will help. A good map from a book store or news agent is, of course, best, but the map available at tourist infocentres shows most major roads. No need to stock up on food and drink, or worry too much about emergency supplies: you're never far from civilization.

🚗 🚗 🚗

Since this is a circular tour, backroaders can begin anywhere along the route. This description begins at the intersection of Royal Oak Road, West Saanich Road, and Wilkinson Road.

Head west along Wilkinson Road.

On your right about .7 kilometres west of West Saanich Road is a trail leading to Quicks Bottom, a marshy area named for the brothers William John and Frederick George Quick, who in the 1890s ran a dairy farm in this area. The trails in Quicks Bottom Park, 13 hectares acquired by Saanich in 1969, are part of Saanich's linear trail system.

For a short walk, continue along Wilkinson Road until you can turn left and park on a side street, then walk back to the path that leads to the park. You can take a circular route, pausing to climb the bird-watcher's tower erected by the Victoria Natural History Society on the north side of the marshy area.

A kilometre and a half farther along Wilkinson Road, a low stone wall on your right signals the grounds of the Vancouver Island Regional Correctional Institute—better known as the Wilkinson Road Jail. Built in 1912 in High Victorian Gothic Revival style, the prison looks more like a toy castle dropped in the middle of an English field. During World War I, prisoners-of-war and those who ran afoul of the Naval Discipline Act were held here. It has been a prison since then.

At the five-way traffic lights beyond the jail, Wilkinson crosses Interurban Road, then Hastings Street. **Turn right on Hastings at the second traffic light.**

A few blocks north, Holland Road winds away to the left, dead-ends on the right. If you are interested in Saanich's wetlands and attendant bird life, turn right, and park to the right of the road. Walk along the narrowing road for a few hundred metres to a pedestrian bridge that leads to a private farm, and look to left and right to see the Viaduct Flats and the birds that use them.

Continue along Hastings Street, then turn right on Granville Street, and left on Charlton Street.

Housing subdivisions end abruptly here. Roadside signs advertise eggs for sale, horses race along the road behind bright white fences, and cattle and sheep graze in the fields. Blackberries overgrow the ditches beside the road, and moss-draped rocks lie among the Garry oaks.

Turn right onto Burnside Road (at stop sign). Bear right almost immediately onto Prospect Lake Road, and continue through ever rockier farm fields where spring lambs share space with dark Doug-

The Saanich Wetlands

The birder with binoculars in the observation tower at Quicks Bottom nods and gestures towards the marsh half-hidden by trees. "Gadwall ducks," he confirms, and writes neatly in his notebook.

From the tower, a watcher can see out over the marshy areas to identify the many bird species that find a home or a temporary resting place here, or even catch a glimpse of a muskrat. At the bottom of the tower, a path winds along the edge of the marsh, where rushes fringe the water.

Quicks Bottom is part of the wet lowlands drained by the Colquitz River and its tributaries. The river runs from Beaver Lake to Portage Inlet, a woodland stream confined originally by the contours of the land and now as well by culverts, subdivisions, and roads. Creeks, including Viaduct, Rithets, and Swan, trickle into the Colquitz along its course. They, in turn, drain wetlands such as the Viaduct Flats west of Quicks Bottom, Rithets Bog, to the east, and Swan Lake, to

the southeast. The river itself runs through Panama Flats, south of Quicks Bottom, a wide flat area wet enough to provide an outdoor skating rink in cold winters, dry enough in summer to be ploughed and planted.

Not many years ago, the Colquitz River was virtually a dead river, constrained by development and clogged with debris. Saanich has since undertaken a broad program to restore the river and build walks along its edges. These wetlands along its course are now mostly protected nature sanctuaries. Various ducks spend their winters and springs at Quicks Bottom; in spring and summer, blue-winged and common teal feed on the marsh. Swan Lake-Christmas Hill is the largest sanctuary in the system, with a nature house, meadowlands, and a lake, each with the distinctive plants of the Saanich wetlands.

The Colquitz River Linear Trail Park, 24 kilometres long, connects Cuthbert Holmes Park, west of Highway 1, to Quicks Bottom.

las-fir trees. **Where Munns Road bears left, keep right on Prospect Lake Road.**

Optional: if you keep left on Munns Road, you can take a short side trip, to visit Thomas Francis/Freeman King Regional Park, named for Thomas Francis, who donated the land, and Freeman King, Victoria-area naturalist. The 113-hectare park provides boardwalks, a nature house, and short and longer trails through the Douglas-fir forest, plus a picnic area and other facilities.

Return from the side trip and continue on Prospect Lake Road.

Victorians have long spent their summers on the shores of Prospect Lake, but since roads to the area have been improved, most of the cabins, cottages and, now, houses, are year-round residences. A number of beach accesses are marked along the road, but most people continue past the golf course, the narrow winding lanes that lead to lakeside homes, and the scrub brush to the playground and picnic tables at the north end of the lake. Not to swim, though—Prospect Lake almost always registers the highest coliform counts in Greater Victoria, possibly because a large number of Canada geese and other birds strut along its shores.

At the north end of the lake, turn right on Eastlake/Goward Road. This narrow road winds between trees and half-hidden houses a kilometre or two to West Saanich Road.

Turn right at the stop sign onto West Saanich Road. Just 300 metres along West Saanich, make an acute left onto Old West Saanich Road.

Though they sometimes seem intended to confuse the traveller, the names of the roads in this area in fact reflect the geography: each road followed trails through the forest that connected farms and village centres.

About 1.8 kilometres along, you'll see the Heritage Orchard on your right, a good place to stop in late summer and fall for apple varieties that no longer find a place on most grocers' shelves.

Old West Saanich Road continues past country properties, small farms, and brushland. The Gazebo Tea Garden, on your left, serves teas and lunches.

You'll reach a four-way junction 9.4 kilometres after you turn onto Old West Saanich Road: straight ahead lies Oldfield Road, a 90-degree left turn takes you onto Sparton Road, and an angle between the two lets you continue on Old West Saanich Road.

Optional route: Sparton Road leads you back to West Saanich Road.

Agriculture on the Saanich Peninsula

"In no part of the country," wrote a provincial agriculturalist in 1903, "is the soil, which is generally a black loam, more fertile, or better adapted for crops of all kinds, fruits and garden produce." His remarks came as no surprise to anyone on the south island: by then, farmers had been tilling the soil of the Saanich Peninsula for more than fifty years, growing fruits and vegetables, grain and hops, and raising cattle, pigs, and chickens.

Twenty-five years ago, the future of Saanich as farmland seemed doubtful. Farmland is flat and easy to build on; suburbs were mushrooming out from Victoria. Then the provincial government declared the Agricultural Land Reserve, preventing good agricultural land from being sold for any other purpose. Both here and in the Fraser Valley, development was curbed and farming continued.

The result of that decision is evident all along the rural roads of Saanich. The guide to farm products put out each year by the South Vancouver Island Direct Farm Marketing Association shows close to forty farms where you can buy products that range from apples to zucchini.

Choose your season and your bounty: strawberries from early June on, depending on what the weather has been like; raspberries not much later; blueberries, peaches, plums, pears at midsummer; hot-house tomatoes and cucumbers almost year-round; organic garlic from a roadside stand; fresh vegetables, from lettuce to beans to peas; brown eggs from a farmhouse verandah refrigerator; apples and apple juice as fall approaches; clear water from an artesian well; honey year-round.

The offerings, though, are not the same, and certainly not the same price, as they were twenty years ago. The

Cyclists ride along Oldfield Road, past farm stands and signs.

The Victoria Region • 13

changing economics of farming have meant that small farmers can't compete in the big markets: supermarkets are more likely to turn to the mega-producers and their mechanized mega-farms in southern California and Mexico.

What the small producers can do, and are doing, is grow specialty crops, flavourful varieties of apples you can't get anymore in the supermarket, juicy strawberries that taste nothing like (thank goodness—literally) the styrofoam mass-produced berries, organic produce untouched by pesticides.

And there's nothing like back-roading from stand to stand, eating your way happily through a summer's day. Herewith a personal Top Ten list, for Saanich back-road farm produce.

- Old varieties of apples from the Heritage Orchard, on Old West Saanich Road.
- Kotata blackberries from Bailiwick Farms, on McTavish Road.
- Peaches from the Oldfield Orchard, on Oldfield Road.
- Venison from White Stag Deer Farms, on Sparton Road.
- Strawberries from Le Coteau Farms, on Walton Road.
- Corn from Silver Rill Farms, on Central Saanich Road.
- Honey from Babe's Honey Farm, on Walton Road.
- Potatoes (six varieties or more) from Hazelmere Farms, on West Saanich Road.
- Blueberries from Bluebeary Hill Farm, off Oldfield Road.
- Artesian well water from Phil's Farm, on Oldfield Road (the farm sells apples and apple juice as well).

Which is not to downgrade the products you'll find at other roadside stands throughout the peninsula. You can pick up a copy of the farm pamphlet at almost every Saanich Peninsula farm. And, thank you, Agricultural Land Reserve.

If you take this route, turn right on West Saanich Road, at the stop sign. Make a stop for ice-cream cones at the ca. 1913 Prospect Lake Market on the corner, then continue on West Saanich Road and rejoin the main tour farther along.

Optional route: Old West Saanich Road passes orchards where you'll find roadside stands packed with apples and plums in season, a bed-and-breakfast or two, and small holdings where eggs are sold. You'll also find a fresh-bread stand. If you follow Old West Saanich Road, turn right at the stop sign at West Saanich Road and rejoin the tour at the corner of Keating Cross and West Saanich roads.

Main route: this tour continues straight, onto Oldfield Road. Spring, summer, and fall, farm stands make the trip along Oldfield Road a pleasure from the time the first strawberries ripen in the fields till the last bottle of apple juice is sold in December.

Continue to the stop sign at Keating Cross Road. Turn left and continue to the traffic lights at West Saanich Road. Turn right. From the junction of Keating Cross Road and West Saanich Road, continue north on West Saanich Road. Optional: west on Keating Cross (it turns into Benvenuto Avenue) is Butchart Gardens, the world-renowned attraction where thousands of tour buses arrive, and hundreds of thousands of visitors walk the grounds every year to see such delights as the Italian or Japanese garden.

Continue on West Saanich Road, past roadside stands in season, and into Brentwood Bay. On your way in, you'll see on the left Sluggett Memorial Baptist Church, named for early settler John Sluggett, who arrived in the area in 1876. The community was likewise known as Sluggett until 1925 when, presumably, someone decided a more euphonious name was in order. Like so many place names in B.C., the new name has a tenuous connection to the province: Brentwood, in Essex, England, was the home of the president of the company that operated the interurban rail line linking the Saanich Peninsula to Victoria.

Optional: if you turn left on Verdier Avenue (watch for Brentwood-Mill Bay ferry signs), you can follow it to the Brentwood Bay waterfront, where you can sit by the dock eating ice cream—or drinking coffee—and watch the small boats heading out to fish sadly depleted Saanich Inlet. In downtown Brentwood Bay are shops, cafes, and services.

Continue along West Saanich Road past the town. Optional: a right on Stelly's Cross Road will take you to the site of the Saanich farm market, held Saturday mornings in the summer. **Continue on West Saanich Road,** and you enter the Tsartlip South Saanich Indian Reserve. The Tsartlip Band has built a longhouse (on your left, not open to the public) and, on the right, the Lauwelnew Tribal School. The fine painted motifs on the school and the totem pole outside follow tribal traditions.

On your left as you leave the Tsartlip Reserve is a native cemetery. The ornate monuments are a tribute to priests who served the reserve, among them Louis Lootens, who came to Vancouver Island from Idaho and died in 1899. These tributes to missionary priests are less poignant than the simple crosses that mark the graves of the Tsartlip, some of them newly inscribed with traditional Tsartlip names added to the English names.

On the left just beyond the cemetery, Our Lady of the Assumption Catholic Church overlooks Saanich Inlet. The classic white country church was built in 1894.

Continue on West Saanich Road, past groves of Garry oaks, farms and golf courses, bed and breakfasts, and gingerbread-adorned houses dating to the turn of the century. The Pauquachin Reserve is about 5 kilometres past the Tsartlip Reserve.

If you want a break from driving, turn left on Ardmore, and follow the signs to Coles Bay Regional Park, where you can sit on the rocks or walk along the cobbled beach. On the corner of Ardmore is the Ardmore Golf Course, the site of a number of Douglas-fir trees more than a thousand years old. The high stump of one tree, a recent victim to time and weather, is now topped by a carved wooden cougar.

The road now curves around Patricia Bay, named for the daughter of Canadian Governor-General the Duke of Connaught, who visited here with her father in 1912. On the left is the federal Institute of Ocean Sciences, home of oceanographers and other scientists who study the waves and tides. On the right is the Victoria International Airport, with the seaplane base across the road and a picnic area beside it looking out over Saanich Inlet.

Past the airport, at the corner of Mills Road on the right, is Holy Trinity Anglican Church, said to be the oldest church in B.C. still on its original site and still holding services. A sawmill on the far side of Saanich Inlet provided the lumber for the church. Yew and oak trees that shade the graveyard were brought from England in 1937, to mark the coronation of King George VI.

West Saanich Road winds past a string of what were built as summer cottages, and are now mostly year-round residences, facing the inlet. Check for handmade pottery in the pottery shop at the corner of Munro Road. On the Tseycum Reserve, a totem pole looks out over the water.

Turn left on Downey Road and follow it to its end, sparing a glance at the farm where miniature horses are raised. **Turn right at the stop sign, onto Madrona Drive. Follow this winding road along the waterfront,** where glimpses of the ocean are visible between old cottages and fancy new estate houses. Turn right onto Wain Road, then look for R.O. Bull Memorial Park on the right. Here, you can walk among thirty Douglas-firs and western red cedars, some of them a metre and a half in diameter and sixty metres tall, among the only remaining old-growth trees in this area.

Return to Madrona Drive, and turn right. The Deep Cove Marina will appear on your left. **Keep right, continue onto Birch Road, and turn left on Chalet Road.** On your left about a kilometre along is one of Victoria's best-known, best-regarded, and most expensive restaurants, the Deep Cove Chalet. People who came to Victoria twenty-five years ago, before the many good restaurants opened, swore by Pierre Koffel and the chalet, in a building erected in 1914 at the end of the interurban railway. The restaurant has kept its reputation over the years despite massive competition.

Stop at the roadside stands to buy apples or eggs; sigh at the million-dollar hideaways tucked between road and water: this area is favoured by those both moneyed and shy. **Turn right on Lands End Road,** and continue between the expensive subdivisions above the road and the expensive estates between road and water. At several pullovers, the road offers good views of the Gulf Islands, with Piers and Knapp islands and the BC Ferries terminal in the foreground.

Continue straight, across Highway 17. Turn left at the second traffic light. Bear right on Canoe Cove Road. This route leads you to Canoe Cove Marina, tucked away from ferry terminal and highway. The Canoe Cove Marina coffee shop is everything a marina coffee shop should be, with coffee (decaf costs more here, as befits such a sissified drink), hamburgers, and marine talk, from 6 a.m. to 4 p.m. To your right before you get to the marina, a rutted road leads to the Stonehouse Pub, a pleasant oasis with hand-hewn beams, stone fireplaces, and leaded-glass windows.

Return to Highway 17 southbound towards Victoria. Take the first exit to the right, signposted for McDonald Park Road. Turn left to take the overpass across the highway, turn right on McDonald Park Road, and continue towards Sidney. This road leads past a clus-

Coffee stop at Canoe Cove, near the BC Ferry terminal.

Walking Sidney

"I don't know where anything is here," says a young friend who lives in Victoria, peering perplexedly at Sidney's main street. "I've never been here."

It isn't physically that far—a half-hour's drive from the city to the town via the highway—from Victoria to Sidney, but for many Victorians, Sidney might as well be the moon. What does it have to offer, after all, that they can't find in the city?

Waterfront cafes and pubs, for one thing. Over the past few years, since development began on the Port of Sidney marina, places to eat, drink, and laze away a rainy afternoon have blossomed on the waterfront. After that, bookstores. And after that, bakeries and clothing stores and fish-markets that aren't part of chains you could find in every other town in North America.

Start your explorations by parking in the Port of Sidney lot (left on Seaport Place from Beacon Avenue, just before the Sidney wharf, almost opposite First Street). Wander around the cafe, restaurant, pub, waterfront walk, marina, Mineral World, at your leisure. If you left your gloves at Canoe Cove, you can catch a water taxi back to that marina from this marina.

Follow the waterfront walk to the right, past said cafes, etc., to Beacon Avenue. Turn left and walk along the wharf, to check out today's fresh fish specials or the ferry to Sidney Spit.

Walk back along the wharf to the museum at the corner of Beacon and Seaport. Continue up Beacon. This main street has a fifties feel: wide lanes good for cruising in your '57 Chevy, lots of free parking, people wandering across the street at their leisure. Up the block north of Third Street, check out Lunn's Pastries for a cross-generational cappuccino and rock

The waterfront walkway in the town of Sidney.

cake combination. Across the street at Tanners Bookstore, take a look at *Motorcycle Madness* magazine or the sailor's charts for any place on the northwest coast. Check out the 1920s post office, or the 1940s bomber round the corner. Have your hair cut at the two-chairs-no-waiting barber shop, complete with striped pole.

And head back to your car quickly—because Sidney does have one big-city attribute: parking patrollers who enforce the two-hour limit on streets and in the port parking lot.

ter of boat havens, among them Tsehum Harbour Marina and the Capital City Yacht Club. You could drop by one to plan how to spend your million-dollar lottery win.

Turn left on Resthaven Road, just past North Saanich School, past Tsehum Harbour. Resthaven is named for a building that no longer exists. In 1912, owners of land on the waterfront here built a private club; it was soon converted, without irony, into a mental institution. In World War I, the provincial government took it over and used it as a convalescent hospital for returning soldiers. After the war, Seventh Day Adventists bought the building and ran it as the peninsula's only hospital, a use that continued until a public hospital was built in the 1970s. Resthaven became a seniors' home, and was then abandoned; it later burned. Resthaven Road takes you past the Sidney library and a fine public rose garden (on the left, just past the library) to Beacon Avenue, Sidney's main street. **Turn left on Beacon Avenue,** to tour the small town of Sidney.

From Beacon, turn south on First Avenue parallel with the water. This road curves to the right beside the Washington State Ferry terminal, where ferries depart and arrive from mainland Washington (Anacortes) and the San Juan Islands.

Turn left at the stop sign onto Fifth Street, and follow this road along Bazan Bay—with views over Juan de Fuca Strait—as far as McTavish Road, approximately 2 kilometres. Turn right on McTavish, cross Highway 17 at the traffic lights, and turn left on East Saanich Road.

East Saanich is another of the original routes that meanders through farmland and new subdivisions. Spare a quick glance to your right as you turn the corner—maybe you should pull over—for the ostriches that graze? neck? gander? in the fenced field a few hundred metres from the road.

Follow East Saanich Road past Panorama Centre and the experimental farm. This Agriculture Canada Plant Health Centre was founded as an experimental farm in 1912. Just before the centre, you can turn left, into a park open weekdays. The farm is a heritage tree area, known for the exotic and non-native trees planted in the arboretum when the station was established. Among them are one of the largest English oaks in British Columbia, a 30-metre-tall English plane tree, and two large sugar maples. Look also for black and white mulberries, planted to see whether the region could sustain a silk industry. Check out the trees in the park and to the right of the road as you continue south.

Ahead on the right is the road leading to John Dean Provincial Park,

Old farm machinery at the Saanich Historical Artifacts Society grounds.

174 hectares of forest and trails. This park, too, has a heritage tree area, with good examples of Douglas-fir, western red cedar, and western yew.

Continue on East Saanich Road. In spring you'll have a view of daffodil fields in bloom on your right, a Christmas tree farm on your left. About 2.5 kilometres along are the Saanich Pioneer Museums, with displays of pioneer life. The Prairie Inn, just before Mount Newton Cross Road, has a long history: a hostelry occupied this site as far back as 1859. Today, you'll find sports fans in the back room, locals enjoying a beer and a bite in the other sections of this verandahed building.

Turn left on Island View Road, and continue across Highway 17. Make an immediate left onto Lochside, following the sign to the Saanich Historical Artifacts Society grounds.

Show up here almost any day of the week and you'll find someone round the back of one of the buildings, probably wearing an engineer's cap, with a spanner deep in the innards of an old tractor or steam pump. Society members seem to work endlessly on this engine or that, creating a spare part from scratch if the sprawling museum and work sheds don't contain one.

Part of the grounds are dedicated to a museum and old steam machinery, with engines, boilers, and pumps scattered around, and a steam sawmill on display. A small-scale railway track circles the other part of the grounds, a big boy's toy for model railroaders who build precise scale models of engines and cars that steam along the tracks. If you're lucky, you'll arrive on one of two September weekends, one the big steam threshing show, the other the model railroaders' demonstration. Otherwise, walk the trails, admire the tracks (complete with trestles), or think up questions you can ask society members at work.

Return to Highway 17, and turn left (south). In just over a kilometre, turn left onto Martindale Road. This can be a difficult turn if traffic is heavy, so be patient.

Martindale Road skims across the Martindale Flats, where different seasons bring different views. In late fall, winter and early spring, water covers the flats in a shallow layer that doesn't quite hide the rotting cabbage stumps. In fall and winter, birders with spotting scopes flock to the flats to identify freshwater ducks, peregrine falcons, gyrfalcons, Eurasian skylarks, and other visitors. In spring, the ground begins to dry and the fields that incline up from the flats turn yellow with daffodils; pickers dot the fields as they cut Canada's spring flower supply. In summer, the flats are usually planted to vegetables or grain.

Turn right on Welch Road and meander through fields shared by

A walker and his dog on Cordova Bay beach.

cabbages and cattle. Welch twists and narrows and becomes Hunt Road; the hedgerows create a feeling not unlike an English country lane.

Hunt meets Fowler/Sayward Road. **Bear left onto Fowler; be cautious since this is a confusing intersection with poor visibility.** Fowler will take you onto Cordova Bay Road. Cordova Bay was long a summer retreat for Victorians, who came by horse and buggy, then by flivver, to the cottages along the seashore. Later, the road became the obligatory Sunday drive for several generations of Victorians, who stopped at Bill Mattick's roadside fruit and vegetable market. Mattick's farm is now Matticks Farm, housing craft stores, a bakery/restaurant, and a plant nursery, on your left after you come down the hill and bear right.

McMorran's Beachside Restaurant, on your left as you continue along Cordova Bay Road, is the heir to an older tradition: there have been McMorrans at Cordova Bay since the 1900s, and the restaurant is the successor to McMorran's Canuck Tea Room, opened in 1919. The restaurant owner still lights a beach fire on the occasional summer night, hearkening back to a time when up to seventy-five fires lit the night in summer-cottage days.

When you reach the traffic lights at Royal Oak Drive, turn right. Royal Oak Drive leads to the tour starting point at the intersection of Royal Oak, West Saanich, and Wilkinson roads.

 ## COLWOOD TO EAST SOOKE

This tour follows paved roads through the Western Communities of Colwood and Metchosin, and into East Sooke. The tour begins in Colwood, as you leave Highway 1 north for Highway 1A and Sooke Road. A loop, it connects to Tour 3 westwards to Sooke, Port Renfrew, and Lake Cowichan, and north via the Highlands Tour 4 to Saanich Tour 1. On its own, it's a good half-day tour, with a stop along the way for lunch. If you connect to the Port Renfrew tour, allow a day for the full journey.

The roads are suitable for most cars and drivers, and for bicyclists, though a better choice for two-wheelers might be the Galloping Goose Trail, along an old railway right-of-way; it covers the territory as far as Sooke and across almost to Shawnigan Lake.

En route are parks, ocean beaches, second-growth forest, riverbanks, farms with roadside stands, camp and picnic sites, pubs and cafes, and craftspeople. All seasons, though heavy rains or snow can make driving more difficult and sometimes impossible on roads subject to flooding.

Before You Go

Any basic map of the Western Communities (Colwood, Langford, Sooke) will show you roads as far as Sooke. There are stores, cafes, and pubs along the route, but you might want to pack a lunch and stop at one of the many parks and beaches.

☙ ☙ ☙

The tour begins on Highway 1A, as it departs west from Highway 1 north of Victoria. **To reach this junction from Victoria, drive north on Highway 1 until you see the signs for Colwood and Sooke. Stay in the right lane here, and bear right, continuing around under the overpass. If you are heading south, follow the signs near Thetis Lake for Colwood and Sooke, and you'll emerge onto Highway 1A, which becomes Highway 14/Sooke Road.**

The twin communities of Colwood and Langford take their names from Hudson's Bay Company employee Edward Edwards Langford, who arrived at Victoria with his wife and four daughters in 1851, to be bailiff of what was then Esquimalt Farm. The farm he renamed Colwood Farm, after his former home in Sussex.

That home must have been in his mind as he played the country squire in his new country: he and his family held parties and dances, open houses and picnics, drawing out from HBC supplies in just one year some 730 kilograms of sugar, and 320 litres of alcoholic drinks. In a single year, he borrowed eight times the worth of his salary from the HBC. Langford didn't last long in his post, but he was not one to take defeat quietly, battling, threatening, and suing until he finally gave up and departed for England in 1861. Enemies of the HBC chose to see him in a kinder light, declaring when he left that he was an "honest, straight-forward and high-spirited English gentleman." Perhaps the writer had been invited to Langford's parties. Both Langford and Colwood are growing bedroom suburbs of Victoria.

About a kilometre from the start of Highway 1A, at the first traffic light, turn south onto Ocean Boulevard. It's signposted for Fort Rodd Hill, but the sign is easy to miss. Then keep left on Ocean Boulevard where the road forks. Just under 2 kilometres from the traffic light, the grounds of Fort Rodd Hill National Historic Park spread out on your left; the parking lot is just off the road.

Fort Rodd Hill was fortified in 1895, part of the coastal defences supposed to guard against attack from the Pacific—perhaps from Russia, perhaps from Japan, perhaps from an enemy as yet unidentified. The defences were declared obsolete in 1956, and the site became a park in 1962. It's now well worth a wander on foot, to see the semi-tame deer that live here year-round, to enjoy a picnic, and to look at Fisgard Lighthouse, the first permanent lighthouse on the British Columbia coast, built in 1860.

Continue on past Fort Rodd Hill, across the bridge that leads to the Coburg Peninsula, a narrow barrier spit of cobbles and sand separating Juan de Fuca Strait from Esquimalt Lagoon.

Continue to the end of the spit and turn right on Lagoon Road. Turn right onto Heatherbell Road, to see a row of Nordman fir trees, natives of Asia Minor, and, at the end of Heatherbell, a cluster of heritage trees planted here in the 1920s and 1930s. **Return to Lagoon Road and follow it to a stop sign.** At this corner is another heritage tree, an old Douglas-fir often threatened by the chain saw because it impedes vision at the corner and always saved by the resulting outcry. **Turn left onto Metchosin Road.**

The origin of the name Metchosin is obscure, though the Coast Salish word from which the name is taken may mean smelling of oil, or place of (fish) oil, or stinking of fish. It is a sprawling rural municipality whose residents fight off attempts to build subdivisions. Always a group to march

Garry oaks in Metchosin.

Esquimalt Lagoon

Some 14,000 years ago, the last great glaciers that covered much of British Columbia were in retreat. Great chunks of ice broke free as the ice melted; some were trapped under moving rock, while others stuck firm in sands and gravels brought by the glaciers when they advanced. The moving and melting ice created many a geological feature we take for granted today, including the Sooke River potholes not far from here.

Such a block of ice, trapped then melting, left the depression now partly filled by the Esquimalt Lagoon, the largest lagoon on the south island. Shaped remarkably like a beaver, with its head at the narrow northern entrance, its tail the shallow marsh at the south end, the lagoon attracts hundreds of water birds and the birds attract many a naturalist. The narrow peninsula between the lagoon and Juan de Fuca Strait is a favourite spot for locals and visitors, who collect driftwood, run their dogs, and enjoy a cup of thermos coffee as they look out over the water and Esquimalt Harbour across the way.

Run-off from the nearby hills drains into the lagoon and out through the gap at each low tide. At high tide, sea water rushes back in, bringing with it some of the sediments the run-off previously carried away. Because of the two-way effect, the lagoon neither fills with sediment nor is scoured ever deeper.

Today's birders bless the glaciers: the lagoon is one of the finest sites on the island for bird-watching. Waterfowl throng to the lagoon from October to May; shorebirds congregate in late summer and fall. Look for great blue herons standing spindly-legged near the north end of the lagoon, and swans, scoters, and ducks that throng near the shore. Sharp-eyed and lucky visitors may also see river otters or perhaps even wild mink at play.

---

to their own drummer, Metchosinites in the 1920s were eligible for an unusual award. The local Farmers' Institute awarded the Metchosin Flitch annually, in an attempt to lower the divorce rate of the Vancouver and Victoria areas, said to be the highest in Canada. The awarding of the flitch followed an old English custom, whereby a flitch of bacon was presented to the couple who could best prove they had lived a year and a day without quarrelling or regretting that they were married. The Metchosin Flitch fell out of favour in the 1930s; if those 1920s farmers could see today's divorce statistics, they might vote to bring it back.

Metchosin Road curves around to parallel the strait; you can catch views across the water over the gravel pit beside the road. About 2.5 kilometres along, a sign on the left points the way to Albert Head Lagoon Park, a small wildlife sanctuary with lagoon and cobble beach. Another

3 kilometres along Metchosin Road is the entrance to Witty's Lagoon Regional Park, a larger park where paths wind down through Douglas-fir and other rain-forest vegetation, past Sitting Lady Falls, and on to the sandy beach and nearby rocks. If you take this half-hour hike to the beach, keep an eye out for western bluebirds in the nesting boxes near the parking lot, shorebirds and ducks on the beach, and seals and sea lions on the offshore rocks.

Less than a kilometre past the entrance to Witty's Lagoon is 'Chosin Pottery, long a mecca for pottery hunters who value the innovative and highly sought-after creations of Robin Hopper and Judy Dyelle. The couple are far from the only potters in the Western Communities, where potters, weavers, woodworkers, knitters, and many another variety of craftsperson live and work. If you can't be here on the late November or early December weekend when much of their work is displayed at the Metchosin craft fair, pick up a copy of the leaflet, available from area tourist infocentres, that maps their locations and describes their wares.

Past 'Chosin on the right is St. Mary's Anglican Church, known as the Easter Lily Church for the carpet of white fawn lilies and purple shooting stars that covers the churchyard each spring.

Continue past Happy Valley Road—or make a short side trip to the right to check out the Metchosin Schoolhouse, open on weekend afternoons, April to October; it opened in 1872, closed in 1949, and is now a museum. If it's a summer Sunday morning, wander up behind the firehall opposite to sample the goodies at the Metchosin Farmers' Market, where you'll find a good range of organically grown produce, and specialties such as bread and homemade sausages.

Happy Valley Road, incidentally, was given its name by or because of blacks who settled here around 1860. Most were emigrants from California, where white gold rushers and other settlers had mistreated them to a degree that made them much less than happy.

Continue straight ahead from Metchosin Road onto William Head Road. This road leads out to the William Head medium-security correctional institution, running past the road to the Lester B. Pearson College of the Pacific, where high-school students from around the world gather for an eclectic mix of studies, outdoor activities, and community service. William Head, at the tip of a comma-shaped point, was the location of British Columbia's quarantine station from 1891, moved west from Albert Head in 1883. Coastal navigator and historian John Walbran noted in his 1909 book on coastal place names that "modern quarantine

buildings to accommodate a large number of travellers have been erected."
A few years later, Chinese returning from World War I European battle-
fields were held here, virtual prisoners though they had worked on the
same side as the Canadians who guarded them, waiting for a ship to take
them back to China.

**Our route, however, takes us just 2 kilometres along William
Head Road,** between sheep meadows where craggy Garry oaks are sil-
houetted, and roadside stands that offer anything from vegetables to raspberries to fresh-baked bread. The road also leads past Devonian Regional
Park; the short forest trails here take you to Taylor Beach, on Parry Bay.

The close relation of Parry Bay and William Head may strike a bell
with devotees of Arctic exploration tales: both were named for nineteenth-
century explorer William Parry. Just round the corner, as the boat sails, is
Beechey Head, named by the same British chart-maker Henry Kellett in
1846, for Arctic navigator and geographer Frederick William Beechey.
Kellett had a strong connection to the Arctic: he aided in the search for
vanished explorer John Franklin.

**Turn right onto Lombard Road, and continue between the par-
allel rows of Lombardy poplars, planted in 1905 and saved in the
1980s when threatened by a new bus route. Continue past grazing
sheep, to Rocky Point Road at the stop sign. Turn left.**

Rocky Point Road meanders past sheep pastures on the left, a donkey
ranch on the right. About 3 kilometres along is Matheson Lake Road,
leading to Matheson Lake Park, 162 hectares of lake, forest, and trails.
A trail from this park hooks into the Galloping Goose Trail, which
continues to Roche Cove Park and on to Sooke.

**Continue on Rocky Point Road, then swing right (with the main
road) onto East Sooke Road.** If you keep left, you'll reach Department
of National Defence land, where would-be wanderers will get a frosty
reception.

East Sooke Road enters the Becher Bay Indian Reserve, part of the
traditional territory of the T'Sou-ke Coast Salish people. The Becher Bay
band runs the Becher Bay Marina, a favourite of the salmon-fishing crowd
in the Victoria area. You are undoubtedly too late to see the fishermen
leave the marina; most are out with the dawn, and returning by the time
the average backroader comes along.

About 5 kilometres from the Rocky Point/East Sooke roads junction,
Becher Bay Road leads to East Sooke Regional Park, the largest on southern
Vancouver Island at 1,423 hectares, much of it still close to its natural

state. This is an ideal location for a picnic. A short walk from the parking
lot leads to the rocky shoreline, indented with sandy or shingle coves;
other short trails lead to rocky headlands. This area was once the Aylard
Farm; you can still see apple trees gone wild and farm buildings gradually
subsiding into the tall grass.

You will undoubtedly also see heavy-duty hikers: a route along the
coast leads to the far end of East Sooke Park, at Beechey Head, an all-day
and moderately difficult trek that becomes very challenging if the weather
turns wet.

Continue along East Sooke Road to its junction with Gillespie Road,
about 2 kilometres beyond the turn to East Sooke Park. East Sooke Road
dead-ends a further 9 kilometres ahead. A side trip to the end of East
Sooke Road allows you to choose the waterfront home you can't afford.
In good weather, you'll wonder why you don't live here; when the rain
slashes down or the wind whips branches from the trees, you'll know
why not. Along the road are some fine Douglas-fir and cedar trees, including one broken Douglas-fir that towers over its neighbours, a fact
important to the eagles who built a nest at the top. Eight kilometres in,
Pike Road leads to East Sooke park and a half-hour hike to Iron Mine
Bay. East Sooke Road here parallels the south side of the Sooke Basin and
Sooke Harbour, a long curved sea inlet that provides protected harbour
for commercial fishboats and private sail and motor boats.

**Return to the intersection of East Sooke and Gillespie roads
and turn onto Gillespie Road.** Gillespie Road crosses the narrow inlet
to Roche Cove, a protected haven. Just past the bridge, on the right, is
Roche Cove Regional Park and an entrance to the Galloping Goose hiking and biking trail.

Where Gillespie Road meets Highway 14/Sooke Road, you have
choices:

• **You can return to Victoria along this road, or cut north on
Humpback Road and join up with the Goldstream-Highlands route
described in Tour 4.**

• **You can continue to the village of Sooke, the old gold-mining
area around Leechtown, and the west coast road to Jordan River
and Port Renfrew, with a possible trip across the island to Lake
Cowichan. For this route, see Tour 3.**

**To return to Victoria or cross to the Highlands: turn right on
Sooke Road.** Two hundred metres along on the left is the Seventeen
Mile House. This and the Four Mile and Six Mile Houses closer to

Victoria are the only remaining reminders of the old coach road that led from the city to Sooke.

Like the others, this "house" is a pub; originally, all were hotels and drinking establishments, stops on the Sooke stage route. The Seventeen Mile was the second hotel in the Sooke area, built as the British Ensign Hotel around 1900. In its early days, hunters from Victoria crammed the hotel full, using it as a base for their deer-hunting expeditions. Long-time proprietor Edith Wilson was famous or infamous: she often refused to serve a second drink to family men she thought should be on their way home to their families, and kept a shotgun under the bar to fend off rowdies. The pub is still a pleasant watering hole.

The origins of the name "Kangaroo Road," on your right 2.5 kilometres along, are obscure; if you stop too long in the pub, you can probably create any number of stories to explain what kangaroos were doing in Sooke. Eight kilometres east of Gillespie Road, Humpback Road branches off to the left. **If you are connecting up to Goldstream and the Highlands, turn left here, and follow the directions in Tour 4.**

Otherwise, to return to Victoria, follow Sooke Road back through Colwood to arrive at your starting point. Garden enthusiasts can stop at Hatley Castle, a further 8 kilometres east from Humpback Road; this former residence built by James Dunsmuir is surrounded by attractive gardens well worth a look. A military college until the 1990s, it is now being converted to regular university college use.

TOUR 3 SOOKE TO COWICHAN LAKE

This tour continues from the routes described in Tour 2, along the paved roads as far as they go west of Victoria, to Port Renfrew. From there, backroaders can return along the same route to Victoria, or cross on logging roads to Lake Cowichan. From the lake, logging roads spear west to Carmanah, Nitinat, and Bamfield; the public highway goes east to rejoin Highway 1. The tour takes the better part of a day.

The paved road is suitable for most cars and drivers, though there are some tight turns and steep drop-offs west of Jordan River. Gravel roads to Cowichan Lake are usually in good condition, though you should inquire locally before setting out, especially in wet or frosty weather. These logging roads can be impassable in snow. The roads to Leechtown are gravel, so take the usual precautions.

Cyclists can make their way to Port Renfrew, though the hills are steep, the road narrow, and some drivers less than courteous.

Along the way are ocean beaches, secluded coves, intertidal life, attractive villages, cafes that are the centre of village life, views, forests. All seasons to Port Renfrew; possible winter problems Port Renfrew to Lake Cowichan.

Before You Go

The *Guide to the Forest Land of Southern Vancouver Island* is probably the best map to take along. Check at tourist infocentres, logging companies, or the Ministry of Forests for a copy. Check your spare tire before you leave, and take along the usual rations. Though there are cafes at Jordan River and Port Renfrew, they may not be open when you arrive; in any case, you may prefer to munch your lunch on the beach or by a river.

✿ ✿ ✿

This tour begins on Sooke Road/Highway 14 west of Colwood, where Gillespie Road intersects with the highway (see Tour 2). To reach this intersection without backroading through Metchosin and East Sooke, take the Highway 1A turn-off for Colwood and Sooke from Highway 1, and continue on Sooke Road about 19 kilometres to the intersection of Gillespie Road. The directions continue on Sooke Road from this point.

Just under a kilometre west of the corner, spare a glance to the left for a partially underground, sod-roofed house. Almost 7 kilometres from the intersection, Sooke River Road leads off to the right. Try some fish and chips or an ice-cream cone at the Milne's Landing store while you consider that this store or a version of it has existed for more than a hundred years; it was founded by settler Edward Milne.

Turn right on Sooke River Road for a side trip to the Sooke Potholes, or just a brief roadside stop (in August) to pick blackberries. The potholes are one of the Victoria area's storied places: many an adult who grew up here tells tales of hitchhiking or biking or going with the family to the potholes, to swim, dive, or sunbathe on the rocks. Though a fence and a caretaker keep out unwelcome visitors, if you walk a short distance up the Galloping Goose Trail, you can look at an unfinished and now decaying luxury resort by the river, another entrepreneur's dream crashed on the rocks of reality.

Return to Sooke Road and continue west. The road crosses the Sooke River bridge. The river has played a central role in the settlement of the area, from the days when the T'Sou-ke first lived here and fished for salmon at the river mouth, to later times when Victoria residents and tourists came to stay at the grand Sooke Harbour Hotel. The Sooke River Hotel and Pub, on the southwest side of the bridge, is partly housed in the stables of the old hotel, which burned down in 1934.

To the right of the road just over the bridge is a display of old farm, mine, and logging machinery, fronted by signs that provide information on the Sooke Harbour Hotel, sawmilling, blacksmithing, logging railways, and the native T'Sou-ke people.

A hundred metres farther along, on the right at the corner of Phillips Road, is the Sooke Region Museum. Moss Cottage, built in the 1860s by the Muir family, sits alongside the museum building. Costumed actors re-create the nineteenth century in summer; displays on the native people, and the logging, fishing, and mining history of the area are features of the museum.

Continue west on Sooke Road, along Sooke Harbour, the centre part of a 6-kilometre inlet. The Sooke Basin is the section farthest east, and the deepest part of the inlet. Sooke Harbour is about 3 kilometres long. Sooke Inlet is a short channel between the harbour and the strait. The harbour has long been a haven and home port for commercial fishing boats.

Continue into the village of Sooke. You can explore Sooke now, or on your way back from Port Renfrew.

The Milne's Landing General Store, at the turning to Sooke Potholes.

Exploring Sooke

The Sooke Community Hall, in the centre of Sooke.

The table for the Rotary Club is next to the one for the Sooke Lions, and just up from the one where students sell raffle tickets to support the school band. You can buy a crocheted lace angel, a second-hand book, a plate of brownies, a jar of honey. Or, upstairs in the community hall, you can find more sophisticated crafts, displayed by the potters, candle-makers, and knitters of the area. Try some honey; buy some jalapeño jelly: it's the annual Sooke Christmas craft fair and bazaar.

The odds are your back-road trip won't coincide with the craft fair, or with All-Sooke Days, the village's major summer event where loggers compete and young kids gobble down cotton candy and hot dogs. But a walking or driving tour can still give you the flavour of Sooke, almost a Victoria suburb but still close to its native, fishing, and farming roots.

You might as well start at Mom's Cafe; everyone else does. Take the first right (Sheilds) past the traffic light; Mom's is opposite the clapboard community hall. Coffee, pancakes, pie; jeans bought stiff and new at the store but now well worn and faded, loggers' boots, baseball caps, truck motor and back-road talk, an old jukebox and pioneer tools: this is the nerve centre of Sooke.

From Mom's take a look at Old Sooke. Return to the Sooke Road and turn right, then left on Maple Avenue, passing the cairn that commemorates Sooke's first white settler, the unfortunate Walter Colquhon Grant, who was not particularly successful at sawmilling, farming, or any other venture in his new home, and who left the colony without the riches he had come for. At the foot of Maple is the Sooke wharf, once the centre of the fishing industry, with fish traps, storage sheds, and brining sheds. Fire has claimed most of the historic buildings, but fishboats still tie up at the wharf.

Return to Sooke Road and continue west to Whiffen Spit Road; turn left. At the end of the road on the right is the Sooke Harbour House, famed for its northwest cuisine and stiff prices. Whiffen Spit cuts across Sooke Inlet almost to East Sooke on the opposite shore. If you go for a walk, watch the tide; it can cut you off from shore. Intertidal life and shorebirds are the attraction here. At spawning time in fall, you can often see seals feeding on salmon returning to coastal streams.

Return to the centre of town for a stroll through locally owned shops; go up the hill on Otter Point Road to finish your tour at the combination bookstore/cafe.

At the main traffic light in the village of Sooke, turn right onto Otter Point Road, and make a note of your mileage: many of the following turns are not signposted.

The following side trip takes you to the site of the old gold-mining town of Leechtown along gravel roads. Five kilometres along Otter Point Road, turn right on Young Lake Road. About half a kilometre farther on, bear right, near the entrance to the youth camp, onto Butler Main (not signposted as such). Just under half a kilometre along Butler Main, pavement turns to gravel. From this point on, until the route returns to this section of Butler Main, the roads are gravel, usually well maintained, but with the bumps and potholes expected from gravel. These are logging roads: check locally to make sure they are open to the public, or travel them after 6 p.m. or on weekends.

At 6.7 kilometres from Sooke Road, turn right on Boneyard Road. Not signposted, it is the first real right turn after the gravel starts, and may be marked by foam plates stuck on sticks, or by trailing surveyor's tape.

Boneyard Lake appears on your left at about 11.3 kilometres. From here on, there are good views down to the Sooke River on your right, with various unofficial camp and picnic sites tucked up beside the river.

At 19.4 kilometres, turn right down a rutted road—or, if you fear for your low-clearance vehicle, park beside the main road and walk in. (If you cross the bridge across the Leech River, you have gone too far: turn back and take the first left.)

This short road/track leads to campsites, usually full on the weekends from April to October, then to the river. On the far side is a maze of old logging roads that criss-cross the Galloping Goose trail, and that lead to abandoned logging sites, to the river, and to the one-time site of this area's largest gold-rush boomtown. At high water, you can only look across to where Leechtown lay. If the water is low enough, however, as it often is in late summer and fall, you can don your gumboots and wade across the river, to explore. Little remains of Leechtown now, though you'll find the equally fascinating rusting remains of logging machinery and old trucks camouflaged by alder, blackberry, and evergreens. If you're lucky, you'll find a loquacious gold-panner, happy to explain the ways of the river to you: try for an inside curve where the water doesn't flow as fast, take a panful from the top of a rock where water hasn't washed away the soil.

Many of those who visit this side of the river arrive from Shawnigan

Leechtown

Sometimes it seems as if reaching Leechtown is almost as difficult now as it was for the prospectors who rushed to a spot near the forks of the Sooke and Leech rivers in 1864. Roads washed out, warning "Keep Out" signs, bridges non-existent, river in flood and unfordable: that's what the present-day visitor can expect.

The reality, of course, is that we have it much easier than those nineteenth-century prospectors. Robert Brown noted his 1864 exploring party had discovered gold "in a locality never hitherto reached by white men, in all probability, not even by natives." Brown suggested the gold extended for 25 miles up Leech Creek, and panning and sluicing it from the banks could employ 4,000 men.

It wasn't long before the first miners were on the stream, building sluices and working the gravel for all they were worth. Tent towns, rocker boxes, thirty saloons, whiskey at two glasses for 25 cents, pack trains, roadhouses on the way from Victoria to Sooke: Leechtown soon boasted what every successful gold-rush town displayed. Except, of course, much accessible gold.

Like many another gold rush, this one soon collapsed: a year after the miners flocked in, most were flocking out.

What's left today? A well-hidden cairn—so well hidden that no one seems to know where it is anymore—a rushing river that dries to almost nothing in the summer, and stories of modern prospectors, as ornery as the old-timers were. Stories are told of shots fired by rivals who may or may not have crossed a claim boundary, and of gold-panners who still take gold from the Leech. But for most of us, Leechtown speaks only in the imagination of the vanished excitement of two brief and booming summers. Almost everything that existed more than a hundred years ago is gone, grown over, picked through by souvenir hunters, vanquished by the rains and by time.

Lake. That road swings west from just south of Shawnigan through the Sooke Lake watershed. Some choose, at low water, to ford the river from the Sooke side with their vehicles and drive out to Shawnigan Lake, but this is strictly an at-your-own-risk activity.

☙ ☙ ☙

The main route returns now to Otter Point Road. To do so from the Leechtown area, retrace your path to Otter Point Road, and turn right. Continue through forest, past a small lumber mill, between farms and stables, through reforested land, until you emerge high above Juan de Fuca Strait; the views here are majestic.

Drive down the hill, and turn right at the stop sign, back onto

Highway 14, now known as the West Coast Road. From here to Port Renfrew, the road parallels Juan de Fuca Strait, now closely, now cutting more distantly across the headlands. On the left, lapping at the windy, driftwood-strewn beach and fronting small cottages, most of which are built on crown land leased to the cottage owners, is Orveas Bay, with Gordon Beach along the shore.

Various four-wheel-drive logging roads angle up from the main road to fishing lakes. But our route continues straight, through forest and past upmarket bed-and-breakfasts that rent rooms for $85 a night and up— mostly "up." The eggs-for-sale signs, however, indicate a much cheaper commodity.

About 8 kilometres from the Otter Bay Road junction is the Shirley Community Hall, the centre of the hamlet of Shirley. You'll have to go far afield to identify Shirley: this Shirley was named for the Hampshire home of the area's first postmaster.

Optional: turn left at Sheringham Point Road, just past the community hall. This twisting, narrow road leads to the Sheringham Point lighthouse, its white and red buildings and the wild, rocky shore it warns of familiar to all who have seen calendars or copies of *Beautiful British Columbia* magazine. You can't tour the lighthouse, but you can walk along beside the chain-link fence and aim your camera through the diamonds and the spaces. Unfortunately, you can't get a clear view since the narrow, unofficial path ends at a sheer drop-off.

Continue west on the West Coast Road. Three kilometres west, a side road leads left to French Beach Provincial Park. French Beach is the first of a series of more or less readily accessible sand and pebble beaches bracketed by rocky headlands. A hundred-metre trail leads to the beach. Because it has both campground and picnic ground, French Beach is probably the busiest of the southwest coast beaches, but it can still be enjoyable. Exploring the tidepools at the western end of the beach (at low tide) or watching for whales are both popular activities.

Continue west 3.5 kilometres to Point No Point, where a teahouse and small resort have stood on the cliff overlooking the water for years. A substantial afternoon tea followed by the walk down to the cove at the cliff bottom have been a feature of many a drive through this area.

Some 3.7 kilometres past Point No Point is the trail to Sandcut Beach. Though a sign exists, brave hunters have slain it with rifle bullets and shotgun blasts, and it lies dead in a ditch—unless it has been replaced. It's standard in this area that signs disappear rapidly, though it's

Sandcut Beach, on the West Coast Road.

hard to say whether regulars want to keep passersby from discovering their secrets, or whether gun-wielding guys just love shooting signs.

The ten-minute walk down a reasonably good trail—the high steps could prove difficult for some, and rain creates deep mud—leads to a perfect book, blanket, and bottle of wine beach, with a waterfall at the eastern end plunging or trickling, depending on the season, over an undercut sandstone lip into a pool formed by waves that roar in from the ocean.

About 3 kilometres farther west, the road reaches Jordan River. One would like to find some Biblical connection here, but, in fact, the place was named for Alejandro Jordan, the chaplain who sailed aboard a Spanish naval ship to Nootka in 1790.

Jordan River was once a thriving community, sustained by logging; it is now closer to a ghost town, though the few residents refuse to give up and move on. Have a coffee and a piece of pie at the Breakers Cafe (if it's open) at the western end of town, and watch through the window as kayakers and surfboarders test the waves offshore. Jordan River is known as the best surfer beach on the south island.

A sign on the way out of Jordan River indicates that the Juan de Fuca Marine Trail is being built, improved, flagged, from here west to Port Renfrew, a several-day journey through rainforest and along beaches intended to complement the West Coast Trail.

Up the hill, around the curves, **just over 4 kilometres beyond the Jordan River bridge, a road leads left into China Beach Provincial Park.** Everyone has a treasured beach, and this has been mine for many years, especially early in the morning, before anyone else arrives. The easy (though in places, steep) trail leads through rainforest where wide cedars and firs share space with ferns and fungi. Below, the surf thunders onto the long shingle beach, and sandpipers chitter through the shallow water. You can walk a long distance east if you don't mind crossing a small stream, moving from sandy shingle, to ankle-twisting rocks enclosing tidal pools, to a distant headland.

Return to the West Coast Road, and continue west. Just under two kilometres from China Beach, a parking lot with red-brown painted wooden guard rails signals (no, there's no sign) the trail for Mystic Beach. The steep hike through the forest leads to another of this coast's fabled hideaway beaches.

There was a time, and not so long ago, when the road west from here was a challenge, narrow hairpin turns falling away towards the steep hillsides, one-lane bridges, gravel, deep U's where some older cars just gave up at the bottom. Some of that still exists, but compared to the old days, the road's a picnic now. It's pavement all the way to Port Renfrew, but newcomers are still advised to take it easy around the hairpins and across the bridges. You may find drivers who know the road well have other ideas, not hesitating to tailgate and pass in what saner people might consider completely unsafe situations. You might just want to pull over and let them go: it's unlikely you'll reform them.

All along the way are informal viewpoints where you can gaze across Juan de Fuca Strait to the American side, where Cape Flattery scales down into the open Pacific. Though no one admires the look of a clear-cut forest, they do allow for views of the water far below—and, as signs along the way keep telling us, the area has been reforested.

Just over 20 kilometres west of China Beach, midway around a blind curve, a rough gravel road leads to the left, down to Sombrio Beach, many people's favourite among the west coast beaches. Most cars make it down to a parking lot, a kilometre or two in, but if you value your car's undercarriage, you may want to park at a pull-off higher up and walk down. Sombrio is known for its contingent of surf kayakers, and also for the squatters who over the years built a variety of driftwood shelters.

A further 13 kilometres on, a short ladder at the left side of the road leads to a 3-kilometre plankboard hiking trail through the forest. **Continue on Highway 14, west towards Port Renfrew.** Two kilometres past the town limits sign, you can turn left to the information centre, both for the area and for the West Coast Trail, which starts across Port San Juan from Port Renfrew. Turn right here to go into town, where you'll find bed and breakfasts and other accommodation, or to make the trip to Cowichan Lake described at the end of this section. Continue straight on towards the real end of the road.

Two kilometres from the information centre, a road arcs to the left and up to Botanical Beach, one of the best-known features of the Port Renfrew area. Zoologist Philip Lambert notes that one could write an entire chapter, if not a complete book on the intertidal life at Botanical Beach. Water has over the years sculpted deep holes in the sandstone, giving rise to tidal pools that contain all manner of sea creatures: brown and red algae, anemones, prickly sea urchins, sea stars, and a host of other plants and animals.

University of Minnesota scientist Josephine Tilden first noted the abundant sea life here in 1901; she started a marine biological station,

Traditional and new at the Port Renfrew Hotel: logs cut for winter warmth, a satellite dish for entertainment.

but lack of access and money doomed her efforts. Since then, countless biologists, students, and others have visited the beach, now part of Botanical Beach Provincial Park. Low tide is the only time to visit, since high tide covers most of the rocks and tidal pools: check tide tables (ask at the Port Renfrew Hotel) before you venture in.

To reach Botanical Beach, drive along the road signposted for the beach until you reach a parking area, then walk in the rest of the way.

At the end of the West Coast Road is the Port Renfrew Hotel. With its boardwalk and canopy, somewhat sagging but still functional, the hotel is an appropriate stopping place for backroaders. Try the pie or hamburgers in the cafe, or drop by the pub for draft beer. Sated, you can walk to the end of the government wharf on Port San Juan—named Puerto (which can mean either port or harbour) by early Spanish explorers. Watch West Coast Trail hikers face their first challenge: manoeuvring down the rope ladder to the skiff that ferries them across the water to the trail, an especially interesting feat at low, low tide.

This marks the end of the road. **Turn back and retrace your route to Victoria—or go down into town, cross the bridge over the San Juan River, and embark on the logging roads that will take you to Lake Cowichan, Bamfield, Carmanah, and Port Alberni.** A note of caution here: some older (and some uncorrected) maps suggest you can return to Shawnigan Lake via logging roads from Port Renfrew. That hasn't been true since 1984, when the logging company that maintains the road blocked off a major bridge that was becoming unsafe.

★ ★ ★

Two gravel logging-road routes continue from Port Renfrew to Lake Cowichan. Before you embark on either, you should check in Port Renfrew about their condition, and to find out if either is closed by active logging or adverse weather. The gravel roads demand the usual respect and emergency supplies. Both routes begin near the entrance to the town of Port Renfrew, on Highway 14 opposite the recreation centre and information centre. Turn west onto Deering Road.

The road dips down to the San Juan River and crosses the river on a narrow bridge. For many months in 1994 and 1995, you couldn't make this trip: high water tore out the original bridge, and replacing it with this new bridge seemed to take forever. A mild annoyance to backroaders, but a major problem for those who lived or worked across the river.

The bridge gives a pretty view of the San Juan estuary; the river and

Port San Juan were named by Spanish explorer Jose Maria Narvaez, who apparently dropped by here on John the Baptist's saint's day, June 24, 1789. **You can continue straight on Deering, or turn left at 1.5 kilometres, to swing through the Pacheenaht Indian reserve and the start of the West Coast Trail.** Hikers who decide to begin at the beginning must be ferried across the river here for a hard-slogging day's journey through the forest. Most choose, instead, to cross Port San Juan from Port Renfrew, and begin the trek at an easier pace. **Follow this road back to the main road west, and turn left, back onto Deering.**

Cross a second bridge and you will arrive at a T-intersection. Turn right for the Fairy Lake-Harris Creek road, left for the Gordon River Road.

Route 1: the Fairy Lake/Harris Creek Road

This is one of the prettier logging-road routes on the south island, leading through second-growth to Cowichan Lake. Paved for the first dozen kilometres, it is reasonably good even in the gravel section. It's the route of choice for Port Renfrewites heading to Duncan for shopping. But watch out in winter: both this and the Gordon River route rise rapidly from the coast, and if it has been raining on the coast, you may well find snow on these roads. Check in Port Renfrew or Cowichan Lake for local conditions before you head out.

When you reach the T-intersection at the end of Deering Road, be sure to read any signs tacked on to the route sign. Both the Harris Creek and the Lens Creek logging roads lead to Cowichan Lake, and one or the other may be closed because of active logging, forcing you to take the alternate route. This tour describes the Harris Creek road; logging company employees at Mesachie Lake say the Lens Creek road is also a fairly good road.

Turn right onto the Harris Creek Mainline. You enter a stretch of road closed in by trees, a favourite thoroughfare in winter for eagles that swoop ahead of or behind your car. Keep an eye out for these big white-headed birds in nearby tall trees and snags. You're much less likely to see a Roosevelt elk in these parts, though elk have been moved here from the Nanaimo lakes area in an attempt to re-establish a resident population.

About 8 kilometres from the intersection is the Fairy Lake campsite on your right, a favourite with paddlers who canoe the San Juan River and with families who appreciate the pleasantly treed campsites. A one-hour nature trail leads through spruce and cedar, though you won't be able to follow it in late fall and winter, when lake waters lap over the shore and into the campsite. Look in the woods for springboard notches cut in stumps from long-ago logging.

Return to the Harris Creek Mainline, and continue east along the lakeshore, watching for potholes as the road surface changes from paved to gravel and back to paved again. The road follows, then crosses, Renfrew Creek, then crosses Harris Creek. Ten kilometres from the Fairy Lake campsite, you reach a Y. **Keep left to follow the Harris Creek Mainline.**

Less than 2 kilometres along this road, on the right, is the Lizard Lake recreation site, another possible picnic stop. The road now climbs into the Vancouver Island mountains, twisting along the contours of the land through Douglas-fir, cedar, hemlock, past ferns, salal, and moss. Some 4.7 kilometres past Lizard Lake, a bridge spans the deep canyon of Harris Creek. In winter, the creek roars over rocks far below; in drier times, it slows to a trickle. Another 3 kilometres along is the one-time site of Harris Creek logging camp. That the old camp area is now occupied partly by a helicopter landing pad says a great deal about changing transportation methods in the logging industry.

About 2.2 kilometres past the landing pad, a sign on the right identifies the trail to the Harris Creek spruce, a Sitka spruce 82 metres tall and 3.39 metres around.

The Harris Creek road intersects the Hillcrest Mainline a further 6.2 kilometres along. The Harris Creek Mainline veers left to the Gordon River camp. **Keep right on Hillcrest (signposted for Cowichan Lake).** Hillcrest climbs a steep hill; this reasonably rough section could be difficult in wet or muddy weather. Thirteen kilometres from this junction, the Lens Creek Mainline departs to the right. If this road is not closed for active logging, you can probably make the return journey to Port Renfrew, though reports suggest the Lens Creek road is steeper and has greater drop-offs than the Harris Creek road.

Straight ahead, you can now follow a wide, flat road to Mesachie Lake and the Cowichan Lake south-side road. Keep right (signposted for Cowichan Lake) 5.7 kilometres from the Lens Creek road (left takes you to Cowichan Lake at Honeymoon Bay) to pass a dryland sort and the timber company offices. If you're lucky, the Skyhook will be anchored here. This giant hot-air balloon is used in an alternative method of logging. On guide lines above a logging site, it lifts logs from a section of cut timber and conveys them high above the ground to a terminal point.

Between 2 and 3 kilometres farther on, the road reaches the community of Mesachie Lake, on the south shore of Cowichan Lake. **Turn right to reach the Island Highway north of Duncan, left to circle Cowichan Lake or continue on to Carmanah or Bamfield (see Tours 7 and 8).**

Route 2: The Gordon River Route

Turn left from Deering Road (see signposts at junction) and continue straight on, past the entrance to the Port Renfrew Marina.

About 6 kilometres from the San Juan bridge is the Deacon and Beauchesne trail, a thirty-minute hike through forest. Beyond this point, the road begins to break up a little, and eventually turns to gravel. **Some 7.8 kilometres from the bridge, keep left across another bridge, this one across the Gordon River, then keep right up the hill.**

The road enters the Vancouver Island mountains, and the terrain changes abruptly. The Gordon River cuts between eroded mountainsides far below, and the road climbs steep hillsides, crossing high, narrow bridges over deep-cut creeks. In places, sudden waterfalls that erupt when

The Gordon River logging road climbs high above the valley on its way to Cowichan Lake.

the rain falls have eroded the edges of the road, and drivers need to be alert for sudden drop-offs. In summer, temperatures rise as soon as you veer away from the coast; in winter, snow falls. The logged hillsides here have been reforested with young trees.

Along the way are signs that indicate logging call points: a logging truck driver can indicate by radio to others on the road where problems might exist, or where he is, by referring to Jack Shaft Summit or Chicken Joe's.

The road narrows to a lane and a half, with pull-outs where drivers can take refuge from oncoming logging trucks. Loggers in this area moved west from Cowichan Lake, so the trees as you go east are larger than those to the west because areas logged earlier were replanted earlier. You now enter Tree Farm Licence 46, a massive piece of terrain where timbering rights have been leased from the provincial government by TimberWest. Gordon River camp, the first logging camp beyond Port Renfrew, was built in 1947, with eighteen bunkhouses, eleven duplexes for families, and all the other accoutrements of modern resource company towns. But once a road was built along Cowichan Lake and into Gordon River, the bunkhouses closed in 1957 and this became a drive-in camp.

If you glance back and to the left as you pass the road leading into the camp, you'll note the loggers' own way of persuading you to yield the right of way to logging trucks: an old wreck squashed almost flat under a huge piece of tree trunk. **Keep left just past the camp, then keep right**, through alder and fir, to run beside huge maples that create a shaded woodland. Continue past Chicken Joe's, a checkpoint that you can create your own stories for, **then keep left about 52.3 kilometres from the San Juan bridge starting point, to reach the Cowichan Lake Road .7 kilometres along at Honeymoon Bay.** Turn left for the circle drive around Cowichan Lake (Tour 7) or for Carmanah and Bamfield (Tour 8), or right to return to Duncan.

SOOKE ROAD TO SAANICH: ACROSS THE HIGHLANDS

A series of narrow, winding roads joins East Sooke to the Saanich Peninsula, snaking through the Highlands area northwest of Victoria, east of Saanich Inlet. Though the roads are paved, they are rarely more than a lane and a half wide; they twist, dip, and climb through fir and arbutus forest, past rocky knolls and camas meadows, and between hobby farms where incurious horses munch hay and dogs sprawl in the sunshine. This tour takes an hour or two, depending on how many times you stop. Joined to the Western Communities or Saanich tours, it can take most of the day.

The only services on this route are at the ends—Sooke Road and Brentwood areas—or where the route crosses the Trans-Canada Highway near Goldstream. Take a thermos or a picnic, and relax at one of the viewpoints or go for a moderately energetic walk from the road to hilltop or waterside.

Not for nervous drivers, but otherwise suitable for most vehicles, though not for large RVs. The narrow roads and steep slopes make it a trial for bicyclists, but not an impossible one if you are in shape and alert.

Before You Go

Because this tour crosses between the Sooke area and Saanich, local maps of each area, available at newsstands and bookstores, will help. There are facilities such as gas stations and cafes near the beginning of the tour, at Millstream, and once you reach Brentwood Bay. Take your hiking boots and a picnic lunch; there are many good trails en route.

These route directions begin on Sooke Road/Highway 14, between Colwood and Sooke. If you are coming from the East Sooke loop, turn right onto the Sooke Road/Highway 14, then left on Humpback Road 8 kilometres from Gillespie. If you are heading west from Colwood, turn right on Humpback Road, 11 kilometres west of the turn onto Highway 1A/Sooke Road from Highway 1.

Humpback Road twists and turns past scraggy farm fields and wooded areas to the cool forest of the Greater Victoria water supply area. Once you're in the water supply area, you are forbidden to leave your car: Victoria's clean water depends on keeping contamination out of the streams that fill the Humpback Reservoir, behind the fence along the road.

Just past the reservoir, keep left on Humpback Road. Follow this road through an avenue of Douglas-firs into the community of Goldstream. At the turn of the century, the elite travelled by train from downtown Victoria to the Goldstream Station, near where Humpback Road crosses the Esquimalt and Nanaimo Railway tracks, then walked or went by horse and buggy to Goldstream Park. These firs bordered the boardwalks along both sides of Humpback near the station.

Turn right at the stop sign onto Sooke Lake Road. Ma Miller's pub, at this junction, is worth a pit stop. **Continue on and turn north**

**on Highway 1, following the highway to Goldstream Provincial Park.
Turn right.** In spring, this is one of the most beautiful stretches of the
highway, with myriad shades of green highlighted and shadowed by the
angled rays of the sun. In fall and early winter, you'll see bald eagles and
gulls by the river, making a feast of salmon dying after they spawn.

Goldstream is popular among casual visitors, especially in late fall,
when hundreds of salmon return to the Goldstream River to spawn. A
trail along the river's edge—wheelchair accessible—makes it possible to
see the fish up close. Their flashing silver is the only touch of precious
metal you'll see here: though Goldstream was the site of a mini-gold
rush late in the nineteenth century, the find was a small one, and the few
mining shafts in the area are long abandoned.

If you stop in the park (parking lot to the left as you turn onto
Finlayson Arm Road), take a look at the Freeman King Visitor Centre,
with displays explaining area flora and fauna, and walk the short trail
that takes you through the salt marsh at the river mouth. Here and
throughout the park are huge old-growth cedars and Douglas-firs.

Continue north on Finlayson Arm Road. Once it crosses the bridge
across the Goldstream River, this road narrows and twists upwards. Western red cedar and Douglas-fir crowd in on either side, with mosses twin-
ing from the branches and ferns sprouting from the forest floor. As the
road climbs, you'll see a transition to smaller trees, with frequent arbutus
and alder.

Barely 2 kilometres beyond the park entrance, Falcon Heights Road
(unsignposted) branches left, past homesteads and hobby farms, old
cottages and new log homes. This rural residential street dead-ends at a
partly obscured view of Finlayson Arm below.

**About 6.5 kilometres from the park entrance, turn left at the
stop sign onto Millstream Road.** You are now passing through the
Highlands. A 1995 park initiative by the provincial government reserved
much of the Highlands between the road and Saanich Inlet as wilderness
park area.

**A further 3.3 kilometres along, bear left with Millstream Road
towards Lone Tree Hill Park.** Caleb Pike Homestead, an historic site
open in season, on the right less than a kilometre from the turn, was the
home of early settler Caleb Pike, who arrived on Vancouver Island to
work for the Hudson's Bay Company in 1850, and ran his own sheep
and cattle ranch here in the Highlands once he left the HBC.

Past the homestead, also on the right, is a parking lot for Lone Tree

The Coastal Douglas-Fir Forest Zone

Straight and tall, its deeply furrowed bark as good as an identification sign, the Douglas-fir is a familiar sight on the southern tip of Vancouver Island. This region and the narrow coastal plain that extends north to Courtenay hide in the rain shadow of the mountains; the precipitation here is less than a quarter of the rain that pounds the exposed west coast. Here, summers are usually sunny and dry, winters mild.

In these conditions, the Douglas-fir thrives—and with and around it grow a host of trees and plants that are equally at home in this dry and moderate region.

The Douglas-fir is not a true fir tree. Nineteenth-century English botanists were puzzled by it: at first, they thought it was a pine; they then reclassified it as a fir, then a hemlock. It is none of these. Most of its relatives live in Asia, and together they make up the family *Pseudotsuga*, false hemlocks. But by the time botanists came to this conclusion, the tree had been known for too long as Douglas-fir for the name to be discarded.

Douglas-firs can grow more than 90 metres tall; long-lived, individual trees can survive more than 1,200 years. Though fire probably burned through much of this area three or four hundred years ago, some of the Douglas-firs survived; their thick bark can be fire-resistant. But few of these senior citizens survived a less merciful enemy. Douglas-fir was the most-used species in the early lumber and pulp mills of the province. Settlement was also its enemy: the forests and meadows of the south island and

mouth of the Fraser River were soon replaced by farms and cities. Perhaps 1 per cent of the old-growth Douglas-fir that once clothed this region remains today: almost every one of these trees we see today is second- or third-growth.

Douglas-fir forest occupies much of Goldstream park; there are some fine specimens beside Finlayson Arm Road as you climb towards the Highlands and others near the campground west of the highway. A tree heritage area, Goldstream park also contains huge western red cedars, black cottonwoods, bigleaf maples and other heritage trees.

Two of Vancouver Island's most distinctive trees grow only in this biotic region. Garry oaks, craggy, with their bent and crooked branches clothed in dark green leaves that turn deep brown in fall, grow in scattered groves on open meadows in the region. Arbutus trees, broad-leafed evergreens whose red-orange bark peels to leave shiny new bark visible below, prefers bluffs and takes happily to poor, stony soil.

Also resident in the Douglas-fir zone are many spring flowers, among them the blue camas dug by the Coastal Salish for their nutritious bulbs, purple shooting stars, and white Easter lilies. You can find many of these plants in Lone Tree Hill park (see this tour route).

The Ministry of Forests produces a pamphlet describing this, one of the smallest of the province's fourteen biogeoclimatic zones. Check, too, at the nature house in Goldstream park, for further information.

Hill Park. The half-hour hike along a good trail to the top of the hill is especially worthwhile in the spring, when deep blue camas mingled with purple shooting stars, along with the occasional chocolate lily, provide a carpeted foreground to the forests, hills, and glimpses of water far below.

You can continue along Millstream Road to its end, past pleasant patches of forest, farm fields, and a bed and breakfast surrounded by neat split-rail fences.

Return back along Millstream Road to Millstream Lake Road and turn left. A kilometre distant, the road divides. If you keep right, you will be on Munns Road, which winds across the Highlands to Prospect Lake Road (see Saanich Peninsula, Tour 1).

The view at Lone Tree Hill Regional Park in the Highlands.

Bear left, instead, with Millstream Lake Road, ignoring the "local traffic only" sign. This narrow winding road follows the crest above Squally Reach and Mackenzie Bight, parts of Saanich Inlet, past small cabins half-hidden in the woods and bright wildflowers in spring and summer. About 6 kilometres along, a parking lot on the right serves Mount Work Regional Park. A 1.5-kilometre trail leads left to the Mackenzie Bight waterfront, and a 4-kilometre trail goes right, to the summit of Mount Work.

Just beyond the parking lot, Millstream Lake Road ends at Willis Point Road. If you turn left down Willis Point, you'll find a small residential waterfront community, with no commercial facilities. **Turn right back towards the Saanich Peninsula.**

This road used to carve through Department of National Defence property; eventually, the military, residents, and tourers got tired of having the road closed when shooting exercises were taking place, and a new road was built around DND property. What the new road loses in attractive surroundings it gains in directness: just over 4 straight kilometres from the junction, it ends at Wallace Drive.

From here, you can turn right on Wallace Drive, then right on West Saanich Road to head back to Victoria. If you turn left on Wallace Drive, you can continue on to Brentwood Bay, for the services described in Tour 1.

CHAPTER 2

The Cowichan Region

IF YOU LOOK VERY CLOSELY, AND WITH IMAGINATION, AT THE side of Mount Tzuhalem, you may make out a rock that resembles a frog basking in the sun. From that image comes the name that the people who lived there gave to the valley midway between Victoria and Nanaimo. Khowutzun, they called it: "land warmed by the sun." Over time, the name became Cowichan, meaning "the warm land."

As those who lived there knew, the valley was blessed with a moderate climate, rarely too hot in summer, rarely too cold in winter. The valley stretches from the end of the Malahat in the south to Ladysmith in the north, trending east-west along the Cowichan River, and north-south along the Strait of Georgia.

The Cowichan region takes in more than the valley. It extends west to the Pacific, covering Cowichan Lake and the forest lands beyond. Some 3,373 square kilometres in size, it ranges from gentle farmland to mountains to rocky ocean cliffs and sandy beaches.

The region contains both gently wandering paved back roads that used to be main routes connecting settlements, and more rugged gravel logging roads built to allow logging companies access to timber. The paved roads are mainly near the east coast; the gravel roads lead overland to the west.

Resources

Most of the maps and books mentioned at the end of the introduction to this book cover the Cowichan Valley. The *Guide to Forest Land of Southern Vancouver Island* covers the logging roads in this region. Also useful are the *Duncan Forest District Recreation Map* produced by the Ministry of Forests (use with caution: some routes are out of date); and the *Community Map of South Cowichan* and *North Cowichan*, published by LRH Ventures, available in local stores. It shows the Cowichan Valley (with detailed maps of towns from Duncan to Port Renfrew).

SOUTH COWICHAN VALLEY

A circle tour, approximately 150 kilometres long, on paved roads (one short side trip on gravel) around Shawnigan Lake, Cobble Hill, Cowichan Bay, and the back roads south of Duncan. The route description starts and ends at Mill Bay on the Trans-Canada Highway, but drivers can choose any starting point on the circle. You can drive north from Victoria over the Malahat or south from Nanaimo—or, if you are a confirmed backroader, you can connect from the Saanich Peninsula (see Tour 1) via the Brentwood Bay—Mill Bay ferry. Though you can easily drive these routes in an afternoon, it's more pleasant to set aside a day if you're coming from Victoria or Nanaimo.

Most of these roads were at one point the main road: in the days before the Trans-Canada Highway, they provided a route for settlers, farmers, and town dwellers through the valley. Traffic in a hurry now takes the highway, leaving the side roads to the leisurely traveller.

Suitable for all cars and drivers, and for cyclists: organized cycle tours can sometimes be seen pedalling these roads, then making the connection to the Saanich peninsula via the Mill Bay ferry to Brentwood. The route parallels lakeshore and seaside, farm fields and forest. This is a roadside nibbler's dream: en route are one cider-maker and three farmgate wineries; markets offering organic produce, fresh bread, and other delicacies; coffee shops overlooking the lake and the ocean. Also along the way are marinas, docks, bird-watching, small village centres, rural farm stands, and historic churches.

Before You Go

These roads are quite straightforward, but a map never hurts. Pick up a free map from a Cowichan Valley infocentre, or buy an area map at local drugstores or stationers.

☙ ☙ ☙

Begin where the Shawnigan Lake-Mill Bay Road cuts west from the Trans-Canada Highway in Mill Bay. Turn west onto this road and

head towards Shawnigan Lake. Mill Bay is increasingly busy these days as improvement of the north-south highway encourages development, and more people commute north to Duncan or south to Victoria. Leave behind the commercial centre and drive west, between developments for mobile homes and new houses and fields where Holsteins pasture.

Just over 2 kilometres from the highway, turn right onto Cameron Taggart Road. About 2 kilometres along this road, through more dairy-farm fields, turn right on Merridale Road, and continue to the Merridale Ciderworks. Don't get discouraged: the ciderworks is at the end of this gravel lane, in a somewhat unprepossessing building.

Al Piggott runs Merridale, the only farmgate ciderworks on the island. In the early days, most of the litre and half-litre bottles of scrumpy and pale golden cider were carried off by visiting cider-philes; now, Piggott supplies keg and bottled cider to many south Vancouver Island pubs and a few favoured retail outlets. Piggott, an emigrant from cider-loving Somerset, is usually on hand Monday to Saturday, 10:30 a.m. to 4:30 p.m., to pour a sample, tell you about the roadblocks to successful cider-making, and express his opinion about mass-produced ciders (the words "horse piss" figure prominently here).

Retrace your route to the Shawnigan Mill Bay Road. Directly across from Cameron Taggart Road, Kees Langhout plies his trade as he has here for two decades, making sausages, smoking ham and bacon,

Al Piggott poses with a bottle of cider at Merridale Ciderworks.

Summer Weekending at Shawnigan Lake

The ladies with their parasols, the men in their white flannels, climbed down from the Saturday afternoon train from Victoria. Here they would spend their weekend, some at the Shawnigan Lake Hotel, others at the palatial Strathcona Hotel down the lake. For all, there would be dining and dancing until the small hours of the morning, followed by a Sunday spent lolling in the hotel, walking in the gardens, or drifting along the lake.

Shawnigan Lake at the turn of the century boasted a fine weekender's social life at the two hotels. The Strathcona Hotel—where the Maxwell Baha'i School is now—was built in 1901, in such a style that many later comers thought it must be a Canadian Pacific Railway Hotel; the CPR was famed for its ornate, luxurious, chateau-style hostelries. But it was, in fact, owned by someone else until the CPR bowed to the inevitable and took it over around 1916. Bevelled mirrors, chandeliers, five open fireplaces, high ceilings, moose heads on the walls, brass beds: all were features of the Strathcona. A floating bridge linked the Strathcona to the point across the shallow bay.

The Shawnigan Lake Hotel replaced an earlier hotel that burned down in 1902. Photographs show it, fancy with balconies and verandahs and elegant ladies in long skirts shading their complexions from the sun. From 1910 on, the hotel was the headquarters for the annual regatta, which featured such events as the four-oared lapstreak race, with boats crewed by three ladies and one gent.

Dining and dancing were not the only attractions for weekend or summer visitors. Other archival photos show triumphant hunters with deer they have shot, or happy anglers dangling trout taken from the lake.

---

and selling these and other meats at the Dutch Deli. Long-time island residents remember the Dutch Deli from its days in downtown Victoria, and a brief stint in Colwood.

Continue on the Shawnigan Mill Bay Road towards Shawnigan Lake, keeping an eye out for farm stands in season. Near the four-way stop sign in Shawnigan Lake village, the decades-old Aitken and Fraser store has been joined by a number of new businesses that testify to the area's increasing popularity with year-round and summer residents. **Stop to shop, or continue straight on after the four-way stop sign, and bear left with the road past the Esquimalt and Nanaimo Railway stop.** The E&N was completed from Victoria to Nanaimo in 1886. Shawnigan had attracted little attention till then, but the railway encouraged development: a hotel was soon opened, and fishermen showed up to tempt the lake's trout—as they still do today. The lake was a very popular spot: on weekends excursion trains brought hundreds of people north. A somewhat truncated train still runs today—one or two self-propelled cars, Victoria to Courtenay and return—but few disembark at Shawnigan.

Continue on Heald Road, past various bed and breakfasts, **turn left at the stop sign on Elford, then right at the next stop sign onto Shawnigan Lake Road.** Just over 2 kilometres along (obey speed-limit signs in this area: police are serious about enforcement), the road nears the lake, and you'll pass the Maxwell International Baha'i School. The school began life as Strathcona Hotel then became Strathcona Lodge School, a private girls' boarding school. In 1950, it became a hotel again, then a girls' school once more in 1959. Later, it stood empty for a time as various retirement home and condominium schemes were proposed and turned down, then became the area centre for Baha'i, a religion founded in the nineteenth century that emphasizes the value of all religions, the spiritual unity of all people, and world peace. Baha'i adherents from around the world visit the school.

Just past the school, bear right with Shawnigan Lake Road (don't go up the hill on the main road). On this right fork, the original road now bypassed by a wider, straighter road, is "The Strip," a row of tightly packed cottages hanging over the lake and known for many years as the summer party place. At the start of the strip is The Galley: coffee shop, docks, boat rental, seaplane base, and water-ski shop. Stop for a coffee and a piece of pie and watch the lake traffic roar by: Shawnigan gets noisier every summer, with jet skis the latest villains now that unmuffled boats have been banned from the lake. Watch for water skiers. Some of Canada's best have learned their craft at Shawnigan, and the ski club has its headquarters around the point across from The Galley.

Turn right at the stop sign, and continue on Shawnigan Lake Road, past the Easter Seal Camp. The road winds between lakeshore and forest; moss-laden fir and cedar, and groves of arbutus and maple reveal and conceal the lake. Offshore is Memory Island, established in 1945 as a provincial park, donated to the province as a memorial by the families of two men killed in World War II. Trails wind through the park, reachable only by boat.

Just under 5 kilometres from The Strip, at the end of the lake, turn right onto West Shawnigan Lake Road. This road continues the circle around the 8-kilometre-long lake. Interestingly, the lake bed here belongs to Canadian Pacific, part of the original land grant included in the package the Canadian Pacific Railway gained in return for building the E&N railway.

On the west side, as on the east, older, more modest cottages alternate with palatial new dwellings. The influx of moneyed newcomers has sometimes caused problems, as they lobby for facilities such as a recreation centre that raise taxes to a level the old-timers can ill afford.

Continue to Shawnigan Lake Provincial Park, just under 7 kilometres from the junction, where you can stop for a picnic, a swim, an hour's fishing, or contemplation of the Douglas-fir and western red cedar that edge the open areas. **Continue along the west arm of the lake to the stop sign at Renfrew Road.**

Until 1984, you could drive between Shawnigan Lake and Port Renfrew on logging roads, stopping to admire the sway-bellied wooden road bridge you crossed about halfway along. That bridge has now been closed, cutting the route. You can, however, make a short side trip west on Renfrew Road to see one of Canada's highest railway bridges, now long out of service but still impressive.

Optional: turn left on Renfrew Road, and drive just under 1.5 kilometres to where the road crosses the old CNR right of way. Park on the left and walk along the right of way to the right, to reach the Kinsol Trestle, a fine assemblage of timber that carried the railway across the Koksilah River. Or, continue on to Koksilah River Provincial Park, for a quick dip in the cold river, or a pause on the river rocks. The gravel road continues to the now-closed bridge, with four-wheel-drive side roads to fishing spots such as Weeks Lake.

From the junction of West Shawnigan Lake Road and Renfrew Road, turn east and follow Renfrew Road on around the lake. About 4 kilometres from the junction on the left is the Shawnigan Lake School. The private boarding school was founded in 1913, and promptly enrolled four boys, two girls. A boys' school for much of its life, it has now returned to its roots, accepting students of both sexes. It is known as one of the brighter lights among Canada's private schools. On the right, opposite the school entrance, is the Reed Crewhouse, base for the school's rowing crews, who have through the years excelled at national and international rowing meets.

Continue around the lake, past Mason's Store, where generations of lakers gathered for coffee and conversation. Regrettably, Mason's no longer has its sit-down coffee bar.

Cross the railway tracks and turn left onto Shawnigan Lake

Road. Just over 4 kilometres from the junction, a number of roads branch right; follow Fisher Road to visit the village of Cobble Hill. There are no known cobblestones in Cobble Hill, nor was it founded by a Mr. Cobble (or, for that matter, a Mr. Hill). In fact, no one really knows how Cobble Hill got its name: perhaps from a phantom Lieutenant Cobble, RN, or, as so many other area names, after an English former home, or even for gravel hills nearby.

Cobble Hill boasts of the oldest annual fall fair in B.C.: if you're in the neighbourhood late in August, take a look. Otherwise, you can shop for antiques in village stores, have a drink in the pub, or stop in for a haircut at the classic village barbershop.

Continue on Cobble Hill Road. About 1.5 kilometres along on your left is Silverside Farm, a must-stop in raspberry or blueberry season, July to August. The farm owners say the special flavour of their blueberries comes from the soil composition here. Whatever the reason, they're something special, as are the raspberry jams, vinegars and syrups for sale.

A kilometre farther on, cross the Trans-Canada Highway at the light, and continue on Cowichan Bay Road. Along either side of the road and on side roads, you'll find farm stands and signs, offering products such as asparagus in April, roasting chickens year-round, garlic through the summer, and apples in October. Keep an eye open for signs. Four kilometres along this road is Cowichan Bay, a 2-kilometre stretch of coffee shops, wharves, cottages on pilings teetering out over the tidal flats, marine supply shops, and community attractions. Undoubtedly, the best way to see Cowichan Bay is on foot, wandering into coffee shop or pub, along the docks or into the fish store as the mood strikes. Park along the road, or continue through the village to a parking lot beyond the stores and cottages, at the boat-launching ramp beside Hecate Park, on the right side of the road.

Continue north on Cowichan Bay Road, past the lumber dock on your right. About 2.5 kilometres past Hecate Park, at a small pull-out on the left, plaques and cairns commemorate the first white settlers in the Cowichan Valley, pioneer women in the valley, and bard Robert Service, who worked briefly in the Cowichan Valley and is said to have published his first poem in a Duncan newspaper before he moved north to the Yukon and wrote the poems that made him famous.

The first white settlers in the valley arrived on August 18, 1862, aboard HMS *Hecate*. They were a little late: four years earlier, in the midst of gold-rush excitement, speculators had bought up almost 4,000 hectares

A Walking Tour of Cowichan Bay

Along the docks at Cowichan Bay.

The waitress at the Bluenose Coffee Shop yawns and apologizes. "Had to get up at four to milk the cows," she says, "then start my shift here at eight." By now, morning coffee time for slackers like us, she's put in close to a full day's work. Meanwhile, the Bluenose owner is having a cup of coffee himself at a table of regulars, arguing the pros and cons of keeping a live-crab tank at dockside, ready for dinner orders. What with the cost and the problems of cleaning off the darn barnacles and seaweed, he's not at all sure it's worth it.

Encounters like this make Cowichan Bay different from pure tourist towns: this is still a working village, not just a tourist attraction.

To explore Cowichan Bay on foot, start at the north end of the village, where cottages are perched out over the tidal flats on pilings; at low tide, the attached docks are high and dry. Stop at the Cowichan Bay Arts Guild Gallery to see what's available by way of pottery or paintings, then wander down onto the adjacent docks for a look at some of the liveaboards and houseboats moored at the docks.

Continue past the Bluenose to the next set of docks and walk out through the Maritime Centre run by the Cowichan Bay Wooden Boat Society. Eclectic exhibits here include old wooden boats, archival photographs, old fishing gear, and displays on the maritime history of the area.

Beyond the heritage displays is the Marine Ecology Station, open weekends spring and fall, daily noon to 6 p.m. in the summer. Even when the centre is closed, you can take a look at purple and orange sea stars clinging to the dock pilings.

Return back to the road, and continue along past cafes, restaurants, craft studios, a fish market, a pub, and a shipyard. The Masthead Restaurant is housed in the old Columbia Hotel, built ca. 1868. You can follow the road as far as the Kilpahlus Resort, then return back to your car.

of valley land, hoping to sell it to people who wanted to farm. The settlers who arrived in 1862 made up the first large group of farmers; from that date on, there was a steady flow of would-be farmers into the district.

Five hundred metres farther on, where Cowichan Bay Road turns left, the South Cowichan Lawn Tennis Club occupies the southwest corner. Grass-court tennis has been played at Cowichan since 1887, making it, members claim, the second-oldest lawn tennis club in the world, just ten years younger than Wimbledon. The grass courts here will never be replaced by concrete or asphalt: the pioneer family that donated the property did so for as long as the grass courts exist. If they go, the land reverts to the family heirs. The club is the last surviving lawn-tennis club on the Pacific coast of Canada or the United States, and among the last in North America.

If you are passing by in June or July, you may be able to catch a set of the action at masters' (over 35) tournaments that attract players from across the Pacific Northwest.

Across the road from the club is a natural grove of huge moss-festooned bigleaf maple trees.

Past the tennis club, continue straight onto Tzouhalem Road. The Koksilah River flows into the Cowichan just west of Tzouhalem Road. The joined rivers flow into Cowichan Bay by way of two main and a number of minor channels, forming a wide, flat delta area, with muddy flats left bare by falling tides. One of the meanings for Cowichan is "river with two mouths," though most ethnologists seem to prefer the "warm land" meaning. Whatever the origin of its name, the Cowichan River has long provided sustenance to the Cowichan Coast Salish, and you may see native people fishing near the bridges.

The river estuary provides for other species as well. **Turn right 200 metres from the stop sign, onto a private road (always open, at your own risk, as far as the gate) that leads to the Cowichan Bay lumber docks.** A number of the 200 bird species resident in or visitors to the Cowichan Valley can be seen along the river channels or in the trees on either side of the road. Waterfowl, shorebirds, and predators frequent this area; nesting boxes have been placed in trees near the lumber docks gate. Look here for bald eagles perched atop trees, or, more rarely, owls, falcons, and English skylarks.

Return to Tzouhalem Road and continue north. A few hundred metres on, farmlands span the road. Wintering trumpeter swans can often be seen here, munching on pasture and leftover crops. The road enters the Cowichan Indian Reserve; property bordering the road should only be entered with band permission. Ask if you may follow the pathway to an old stone church, at the top of a hill 2 kilometres past the start of Tzouhalem Road. Look for a small pull-off on the left side of the road, beside a path that winds to the top of the hill. The Stone Church, now abandoned but its 50-centimetre-thick stone walls still picturesque, was built by the Cowichan in 1864, paid for with butter sales—hence its alternate name, the Butter Church.

Behind the church rises the bulk of Mount Tzuhalem, named for a war chief of the Cowichan, banished by his people because of his violent acts. Chief Tzuhalem went to live in a cave on the mountainside.

A little over a kilometre ahead on the right is the fourth church to carry the name St. Ann's. The first was a log church that predated the Butter Church; the Butter Church was the second. Each served for a decade as the mission church of the Oblate fathers and the Cowichan native

people. The third building was erected after authorities decided that the church should be on church-owned land. This fourth church, dating from ca. 1900, was repainted a number of years ago, and the interior reflects the colours of the surrounding forest.

Just past the church on the right, a road leads to what was for many years St. Ann's residential school, run by the Sisters of St. Ann, who first came to Vancouver Island from Quebec in 1858. The buildings and surrounding land are now Providence Farm, a com-

St. Ann's Church, near Cowichan Bay.

munity facility that employs valley people with various disabilities. Drop by in season—spring to fall—for a taste of the farm's specialties: basil, which fills a greenhouse and shows up on the tables of many local restaurants, and varieties of peppers.

Continue along Tzouhalem Road. A further 1.2 kilometres along on the right is St. Peter's Quamichan Anglican Church, a frame church built in 1876 and still used.

Turn left onto Trunk Road at the stop sign. One of the trees at this junction was reputed to be a hangman's tree, where possibly a chief, or maybe a slave, was hanged in 1856 for shooting and seriously wounding a white settler who had seduced the Indian's future bride. While some swear this is the location, others suggest it was far away, and that the tree used is unknown—a suggestion that gains credence when you look at the rather spindly Garry oaks here.

Continue west on Trunk Road, through the traffic lights at Highway 1 and into the centre of Duncan. Turn left onto Allenby Road at traffic lights. Cross the river and continue straight ahead at the stop sign onto Indian Road. This route takes you into the pleasant farming and wooded country southwest of Duncan, and the hamlet of Glenora.

Stop for a moment at the Community Farm Store (**stop sign, corner of Indian, Glenora, and Marshall roads**). This outlet for Altemueller's Biodynamic Farm sells wondrous bread, and such delights as Heritage tomatoes and fresh walnuts. The biodynamic farm (**straight ahead on Marshall Road**) sometimes has a stand of its own on the driveway leading to the old homestead and ca. 1900 farmhouse.

The farm is part of a movement that stresses that each farm is a unique ecosystem that should be as self-sufficient as possible, using manures and composts, working within a balanced system that extends from plants, animals, and soil to the rhythmic workings of the stars and planets. Those interested in the concept can ask for information at the Community Farm Store.

If you are ready for a walk, **turn right at the stop sign and follow Vaux Road to Robertson Road; turn right and drive to a parking area opposite the Cowichan Fish and Game Club grounds.** Walk in through the gate to find the beginning of the Cowichan River Footpath, first developed by anglers as a way to reach the steelhead pools along the river, which leads 19 kilometres from here along the river and on to Lake Cowichan.

Return to the four-way stop, and turn right on Marshall Road to Vignetti-Zanatta Winery, a hundred metres ahead on the left.

Return to the Glenora/Marshall/Indian roads intersection, and head southeast (away from the stores) on Glenora Road, which ambles between sheep and lamb pastures, barns, and bright new housing that indicates Duncan suburbia is spreading south. **About 3.5 kilome-**

Wineries of the Cowichan Valley

Loretta Zanatta pours a cool taste of Ortega wine for the visitor, and remembers the first day she sold wine at the Vignetti Zanatta (the Zanatta vineyard). She had got married the week before and came back from her honeymoon to discover the labels for the wine had just arrived. She, her parents, and her two sisters worked through the night getting ready for the next day's sales. When they opened the door the next morning, they saw a long line-up stretching towards the road. "We had no idea what it would be like," she says, still incredulous.

Dionisio Zanatta came to Canada from Italy, worked with stone tile and terrazzo, then bought this dairy farm near Glenora. Interested in grapevines, he planted different varieties on the farm. In 1986, anticipating new licensing regulations that would allow him to sell wines at the farmgate, he planted two hectares of grapes. Today, the family winery produces dry, white Ortega, sparkling Glenora Fantasia brut, and white Auxerrois that they sell at their farmgate winery. Taking advantage of new farmgate regulations, in summer they run an *enoteca* in the old farmhouse, where visitors can eat and sample wines made on the premises.

Vignetti Zanatta is one of four farmgate wineries that now operate in the Cowichan Valley. At first glance, Vancouver Island's cool summers may seem less than ideal for growing good wine grapes. But the Cowichan Valley, with its long warm summers and mild winters, is gaining a name as a wine-making region.

A chronicler of the Cowichan Valley recounts that one early settler made moonshine liquor that he called wine, a pale beverage that burned the throat and warmed the soul. The settler lived near Cherry Point, so that would make Wayne and Helena Ulrich and their Cherry Point Vineyards the second vintners near this spot.

The Ulrichs are fervent experimenters; at one side of their vineyard are patches of various grape varieties they are testing for possible future production. Now, they make Gewurztraminer and the island's only Pinot Blanc. Not far from Vignetti-Zanatta is Blue Grouse Vineyards, where wine-maker Hans Kiltz specializes in German-style white wine. And just off the highway near Cobble Hill is Venturi-Schulze, producing fine wines and balsamic vinegar.

Vignetti Zanatta, Cherry Point, and Blue Grouse are open at posted hours, and welcome wine samplers and purchasers. Venturi-Schulze has more limited hours, usually by appointment.

tres along, turn right at the stop sign, onto Miller Road. Just beyond, turn right at a second stop sign onto Koksilah Road.

Some 2.3 kilometres along, you'll see on the right a small cairn and plaque that commemorates an almost-forgotten event between World War I and II, when poor British children were sent to the dominions for a fresh start. The Fairbridge Farms in Canada and Australia took in a number of these children, teaching the boys farming and the girls house-hold skills. Some 328 children attended this farm school between 1935 and 1948. The area is now part farm, part housing development.

Continue along Koksilah Road, across the river, and past Cowichan Station Road. To visit a second winery, turn right at Lakeside Road (6 kilometres from the Miller Road/Koksilah intersection), then turn right a kilometre later into Blue Grouse Vineyards and winery, open on Wednesday, Friday, Saturday and Sunday, 11 a.m. to 5 p.m.

Return to Koksilah Road and continue east, past an ostrich farm— these creatures bid fair to be in the 1990s what silver foxes were in the 1930s—and cross Highway 1 at the traffic lights. Just down the road is Wilding Heritage Farm, an operation dedicated to the survival of en-dangered breeds of farm animals. Concerned by the trend towards agri-business that standardizes farm breeds, the owners of this farm breed and raise some sixteen types of cattle, pigs, sheep, goats, and chickens, among them Canadienne cows that date back to sixteenth-century New France and Tamworth pigs, one of the oldest breeds of swine. Check the sign for hours when visitors are welcome.

Continue on Koksilah Road. Cross Cowichan Bay Road at the stop sign, and continue straight on Cherry Point Road, as it curves south then west. The third of the valley wineries, Cherry Point Vineyards, run by sociable and knowledgeable owners Wayne and Helena Ulrich, is 6 kilometres from Cowichan Bay Road, on the right: look for the wine barrel at the roadside and stop in for a taste of Pinot Blanc and other Cherry Point specialties.

A kilometre past Cherry Point, turn left on Telegraph Road at the stop sign. This road passes Arbutus Ridge, a contained community for over-fifties, complete with golf course and indoor tennis courts. Along this road in season, you'll find stands offering for sale such delicacies as salsa, quiche, brown eggs, and free-range chickens.

Turn right at the stop sign onto Kilmalu Road. This will take you back to Highway 1; turn left at the traffic lights to return to the tour starting point in Mill Bay.

 **NORTH COWICHAN VALLEY**

A variable tour, from 70 to 80 kilometres long, depending on route and side trips, from Duncan north through Chemainus to Ladysmith, or to Chemainus then back to Duncan along the back roads and west of the Trans-Canada Highway. Almost all the route is suitable for all vehicles, drivers, and cyclists. Only the side trip up Mount Prevost is gravel, rough and steep. The route starts at the main traffic light in Duncan, and can be driven as a circle, or as a trip between Duncan and Ladysmith. This is a pleasant half-day outing.

The roads on the east side of the highway parallel hidden saltwater bays or cut through farm fields. Along the way are coffee shops and mariners' talk; rocky woods and farm houses; painted murals and fish and chips; views and rural hamlets.

Before You Go

A detailed map is not really necessary, but you might want to pick up a free valley map from a tourist infocentre, or buy a more detailed map from a local store.

✵ ✵ ✵

Begin at the junction of Highway 1 and Trunk Road, the main intersection in Duncan. Turn east, towards the water, on Trunk Road: a right turn if you are heading north from Victoria, a left turn if you are heading south from Nanaimo.

About .3 kilometres from the highway, stay in the right lane, and continue straight on, onto Marchmont, following the signs to the Freshwater Ecological Centre. Turn right on Lakes Road, and you'll arrive at the eco-centre and the banks of the Cowichan River.

Return to the stoplights at Trunk Road and turn right. Continue onto Tzouhalem Road (no turns, just a change in the name of the road), then bear left onto Maple Bay Road.

The language on the roadside signs here arouses a certain grim amusement, as housing developments take over the rocky meadows and woodlands east of Duncan: you can choose among "adult developments," "hills," "estates," and "terraces," depending on your preference for a townhouse, a massive new mansion, or an empty lot.

You can catch glimpses to your left of Quamichan Lake, with Somenos Lake beyond, pleasant places to relax or do a little bird-watching. But not from here: access is strictly limited from this side of the lakes.

Duncan's Freshwater Eco-Centre

In a tree high above a backwater of the Cowichan River, a trio of herons perches, heads folded down onto their shoulders. Below them, mallard ducks and goldeneyes scoot down the stream with the current, watched anxiously by the leashed dog being walked by its owner on the river dyke path.

This well-used path leads from the Freshwater Eco-centre along the river to Duncan's Silver Bridge. In time, kiosks and viewing stations, erected through volunteer labour and contributions in money and in kind, will present the natural history of the Cowichan watershed. The interpretive walkway is the second stage in a project to present this natural history to valley residents and tourists alike; the first stage is the eco-centre itself.

In the centre, photographs, models, and interactive displays give visitors insights into the ecology of the river. Live trout swim in a tank, a hands-on model identifies various parts of a fish, and pictures and words describe the native history of the Cowichan Valley. Children—or interested adults, for that matter—can discover how and why sounds differ in air and underwater, what fish eat, and what eats fish. Slide and video presentations describe the valley ecology.

The eco-centre is linked to the Vancouver Island Trout Hatchery next door. Visitors can see trout at various stages of growth, and discover how the hatchery operates.

The centre is open 10 to 3:30, Thursday through Sunday; July through September, it is open 10 to 5 every day. Even when it is closed, visitors can stroll along the dyke to the bridge. Picnic tables are located near the river just before the bridge.

A holly farm on the right of the road has resisted the pressures of urban development and still ships spiny leaves and red berries around the world. Just beyond the farm is the Quamichan Inn, a turn-of-the-century mock-Tudor hostelry, across from fields studded with Garry oaks.

Some 5.4 kilometres from the beginning of Maple Bay Road, turn right onto Genoa Bay Road. The derivation of the name Maple Bay is apparent; Genoa Bay is less so. It was probably named by Italian immigrant Giovanni Baptiste Ordano, who came here in 1858; possibly a reminder of his birthplace, it makes a nice change from all the area names derived from the birthplaces or former homes of British settlers. Ordano, by the way, opened the first store in the district of Tzouhalem.

The road curves down along Bird's Eye Cove, through craggy rock and stands of arbutus and fir. New houses are fast going up atop the rocks, of a sufficient size that one passerby commented, "These aren't retreats; they're domains."

Below the developments, the gentle curve of the bay, studded with

A live-aboard and its guardians at Genoa Bay.

docks and buoys, takes the eye past a yacht club and several marinas. Live-aboards make up a floating community here, together with yachts, sailboats, motorboats, and even rowboats. Turn left into the Maple Bay Marina to wander along the floats or for coffee, beer, and/or a meal at the Shipyard restaurant/pub.

Beyond the marina, the massive new homes cease, and you drive through a short area of modest cottages and cabins that feel tied to the water rather than dominating it. Beyond the settlement, the road passes between sharp rocks on the right and stony farm pastures spotted with giant boulders on the left. Cedars and bright green moss clothe the rocks to the right.

About 6 kilometres from Maple Bay, the road ends its cross-country journey among cattle, rocks, meadows, and barns at Genoa Bay, which looks south, back towards Cowichan Bay. In the early morning, mariners' chat drifts up from the Genoa Bay coffee shop as boaters discuss weather and baulky engines over endless cups of coffee. This is a perfect place to sit and eavesdrop or daydream over a morning newspaper and your own cup of coffee, a thousand kilometres removed from stress and bustle. You can stroll from the coffee shop to the store and the art gallery that may or may not be open, then check out the float homes, yachts, and other boats that tie up at the docks.

Return back along Genoa Bay Road to Maple Bay Road. Turn right. Continue down the hill through the village of Maple Bay to a

stop sign, and turn right onto Drummond Drive. Turn left at a stop sign onto Beaumont, then continue with this road along the shore. You can park near the government wharf to spend some time looking out over Maple Bay towards Saltspring Island, across Sansum Narrows, another of those geographic points named for Royal Navy men aboard ships used to chart this coast. While many of the men commemorated on the coast never saw British Columbia, Lieutenant Arthur Sansum, RN, never returned to England: he died of apoplexy at Guaymas, Mexico, soon after leaving the northwest coast. The Brigantine Pub and a small waterfront park both provide good vantage points.

For the best views, however, continue along the road parallelling the shore as it curves out from the bay to the narrows. A walking trail on your left a few hundred metres from the town centre leads to more views; 1.5 kilometres along the road, a public beach access leads to the right, just before the turnaround that allows you to retrace your route to town. Here, you can see the reason for the word "narrows": Saltspring Island seems just an arm's length away.

Return to town, and turn back up the hill on Drummond. Keep left on Maple Bay Road, then turn right on Herd Road, following the sign to Crofton. Herd Road leads you north again, through a farming valley where you can pick up brown eggs or produce from roadside stands. **Three kilometres from the Maple Bay waterfront, turn right on Osborne Bay Road. Five kilometres along this road, you will reach the mill town of Crofton.**

A hundred years ago, this quiet seaside pulp mill town was all abustle: At the turn of the century, miners on Mount Sicker, to the west, were blasting out copper ore and loading it on railway cars that brought it to the new smelter at the port of Crofton. The smelter operated for just five years, until the price of copper dropped dramatically and the smelter burned down, equally dramatically. But that was long enough for the usual boom town to spring up, complete with houses, hotels, bars, and stores.

Today's Crofton lives mainly from the Fletcher Challenge pulp mill near town. **Where Osborne Bay Road—now York Avenue—ends at a stop sign, turn right, and drive towards the docks.** A ferry from here connects with Vesuvius, at the north end of Saltspring Island. **Turn right on Queen Street, just before the wharf.** On your right at the end of the block are the Travel Infocentre and the Crofton Museum, housed in a 1905 schoolhouse. Just outside the museum is a wood sculpture, *Adam*

The Crofton Old School Museum and Infocentre.

and Eve, executed by Swaziland artist Johann Mhlanga in 1986, as part of a sculptors' exchange.

You can arrange for a tour of the pulp mill at the tourist centre, or find out about the Cowichan Ecomuseum. The ecomuseum, born of a concept more familiar to Europeans than to North Americans, treats the thousand square kilometres of the Cowichan Valley as an open-air museum, where natural and human history are on display in the midst of everyday activities.

Turn right on Joan Avenue, and head back towards York Avenue, past milltown cottages, cafes and stores that give Crofton its small-town flavour. **Turn right on York, then left on Chaplin, then bear right on Crofton Road about 200 metres farther on. Continue north on Crofton Road,** past the entrance to the Crofton pulp mill. **Just under 4 kilometres from the centre of Crofton, turn right at a T-intersection onto Chemainus Road.**

All these back roads follow the route of old roads that meandered from settlement to settlement, designed at first for horse-drawn carriages and wagons, then for cars and people who rarely needed to travel rapidly. Like the others, the Chemainus Road is picturesque and slow. Cross the bridge over the Chemainus River—photo opportunities here—and continue on between the railway and the ocean towards Chemainus, past cottages, the occasional farm houses, and horses in fields, then past the big old mill buildings close by the road and across old railway tracks that once saw cars loaded with logs arrive at the timber mill.

Chemainus begins about 5 kilometres along the road. Those who don't know the story of modern Chemainus—dying mill town to thriving tourist town—must be few: the determination of townsfolk to keep this town from the fate of a hundred similar boom-and-bust resource towns has made headlines across North America. The earliest white settlers in this area started a timber-cutting business and a lumber mill in 1862. Logging and lumbering expanded over the years. Chemainus companies acquired the first logging locomotive in B.C. in 1899, expanded both mill and loading wharves over the decades, and built a major new mill with its accoutrements.

That sawmill shut down in the early 1980s. Chemainus could have died, but many who lived there wanted to stay. They determined that Chemainus would become the world's largest outdoor art gallery; in the 1980s and 1990s, artists completed some thirty murals depicting area history on town walls. Chemainus is now a stop on many a bus tour, and visitors crowd the souvenir shops, cafes, restaurants, and art and craft galleries. **Continue along Chemainus Road;** on your left a few blocks up is a railway car that houses an information centre where you can get a map of the town that pinpoints the location of each mural and other stops of interest, all best seen by parking your car and walking the streets.

To reach the waterfront: turn right at Victoria Street, at the south end of town, in front of the Chemainus Theatre, then follow

Chemainus buildings decorated for Christmas.

One of the many murals that have made Chemainus famous.

Victoria to the left, down the hill, to Oak Street. Turn right and park. You can walk along these lower streets to the wharf. To the right is Chemainus Bay. Though there are many stories about the origin of the name Chemainus, the most interesting is that it comes from a Halkomen word meaning "bitten breast" and refers to the shape of the bay, said to resemble a bite that a shaman might take out of an onlooker during native ceremonies. Later comers were less imaginative, calling it Horseshoe Bay.

Chemainus now has a new lumber mill. If you are interested in seeing the workings of a high-tech mill that cuts to order, you can go on a tour, June to October, Tuesday and Thursday. Ask at the tourist infocentre for details.

Return to Chemainus Road.

To head north towards Nanaimo: turn right on Chemainus Road. This will become Old Victoria Road—a nod to its origin as the first up-island highway—and lead through the seaside community of Saltair back to the Island Highway (1) just south of Ladysmith. Saltair's Porterhouse Pub, on a side road to your right about 3 kilometres from Chemainus, is in a turn-of-the-century white clapboard house built by early settler Robert Porter.

To complete the back-road circle tour: turn left on Chemainus Road and retrace your route south. Just past the bridge over the Chemainus River, continue straight on with Chemainus Road.

Blackberries almost obscure a subsiding cabin and shaggy ponies nibble grass in roadside fields as the road crosses into the Chemainus Indian Reserve. **About 2 kilometres from the bridge, keep left onto Westholme Road,** to pass through Westholme, a community hardly recognizable as such. Some of the miners who worked Mount Sicker lived in Westholme, a stop on the Esquimalt and Nanaimo Railway line. There's little evidence of the old town now; the road crosses rural country, past red barns standing in fields that flood with heavy rains in spring and fall, small businesses, and attractive houses and farm buildings.

Continue straight on 3.4 kilometres past the beginning of Westholme Road, looking out just past the Y-junction for ostriches on a farm that specializes in the gawky, long-legged, long-necked birds. **Cross the highway at the stop sign, with caution: visibility is not particularly good at the intersection.** You are now on Somenos Road, west of Highway 1.

High to your right, you can just discern a memorial column atop Mount Prevost; you can reach the summit via a side trip on gravel roads, followed by a steep hike.

This side trip on rough roads, which are narrow, steep and winding, and not suitable for cars with trailers, may be impossible in wet weather.

Optional: to make the side trip, turn right 3.8 kilometres from the highway onto Mount Prevost Road. About 2.5 kilometres along, through logged-off land and second growth, is a viewpoint that looks out over the Cowichan Valley, the water, and the Gulf Islands. Just over 4 kilometres from the beginning of Mount Prevost Road, keep left, then keep left again another kilometre along, in all cases following the road that looks the most travelled. This road leads you to two parking areas about 7.5 kilometres from Somenos Road. Park and walk one of the rough trails to the mountain's twin summits, which give you fine views of the Strait of Georgia to east and north, the Saanich Peninsula, Juan de Fuca Strait and on particularly clear days the Olympic Mountains to the south, and the straits and mountains to the northeast. On the eastern summit stands the memorial column visible from below. It was built in 1929, to honour those from the valley who saw military service in World War II. Each trail takes about half an hour to walk.

Continue south on Somenos Road. About .7 kilometres on, cross Highway 18, which leads to Lake Cowichan, then 2.5 kilometres farther on, continue straight on at a four-way stop. Follow on through the traffic lights, to return to the centre of Duncan and your starting point at Highway 1.

 **DUNCAN TO COWICHAN LAKE**

This is a circle tour, approximately a hundred kilometres long, half paved roads, half good gravel, starting
and ending at Duncan. This tour takes the back roads
west from Duncan along the Cowichan River to the town of Lake Cowichan, then circles 30-kilometre-long Cowichan Lake on gravel roads and
follows the highway back to Duncan. The drive takes about half a day,
assuming stops for food, drink, and the occasional walk.

Along the route are forest and foaming river, lakeside pubs and cafes,
nature walks, lake views; picnic and camp sites, hiking, and link-ups with
the back roads that lead to Carmanah Provincial Park and to Bamfield
and Alberni Inlet and valley. The roads are suitable for most cars and
drivers who can handle gravel roads, though the loop around the lake
can be dusty, muddy, or bumpy depending on weather and usage. From
Duncan to Lake Cowichan is suitable for cyclists. In winter, check in Lake
Cowichan for road conditions around the lake.

Before You Go

The route is quite straightforward. If you want to take a map along, the
Community Map of Cowichan Lake (included in the map of South
Cowichan) and the *Community Map of North Cowichan* are useful. Cafes,
pubs, and other facilities are in towns en route. There are lots of places to
walk and/or picnic. The usual gravel-road warnings apply.

☬ ☬ ☬

**Begin at the traffic lights at Duncan's main intersection: Highway 1
and Trunk Road. Turn west onto Trunk Road, towards the centre of
Duncan. Follow Trunk; it will angle right in town and become Government. Follow Government Street.** This route takes you past some
of the best of Duncan's many roadside totem poles, which stand to the
left of Government Street, in front of the seniors' centre and the provincial
government building. The totems are the result of a co-operative project
by the city and native carvers, begun in 1985 and still underway. You can
get information on and a map of the totems at the infocentre on the
highway or at the Chamber of Commerce office downtown.

**Continue on Government Street up the hill, then turn left onto
Gibbons Road.** The road takes you out through a rapidly suburbanizing
area, where a holly farm, old barns, streams, gullies, and cows share space
with new houses, a trailer park, and joggers.

Gibbons passes by the hamlet of Vimy and Normandy Road,

reminders of World War I and II. **Five kilometres from the start of Gibbons, turn left on Barnjum Road,** a fairly narrow, winding, gravel route. **Two kilometres farther on, turn left at a stop sign back onto pavement; this is Riverbottom Road.** It cuts through pleasant farm fields, then into second-growth forest, where alder and brush edge cedar and Douglas-fir. The road parallels the winding Cowichan River, glimpsed far below through breaks in the forest.

About 7 kilometres along is Sahltam Lodge, a fixture in the valley for many years. Walkers who tread the Cowichan River footpath from its eastern end can cross the river here by cable car and have a meal at Sahltam.

The road climbs a hill and angles down again, through young forests that signs indicate were replanted in 1983 and 1993. Fifteen kilometres from the turn onto Riverbottom Road is Skutz Falls, a series of low cascades much beloved by kayakers, inner-tubers, and those who like to see the salmon ascend the fish ladders in the fall. Continue straight on Riverbottom Road: several parking lots exist to the left of the road over the next 2 kilometres, all with trails leading to and along the river.

Continue straight, onto Skutz Falls Road, a winding, dusty route through second-growth forest, past moss-covered tree trunks and shade that promises a good picnic site on a hot summer day. About 5 kilometres past Skutz Falls, you'll come to the old Cowichan Lake Road, just before Highway 18.

Optional: to return to Duncan, turn right, and follow the old road through forests and farm fields. Turn right at the stop sign in 16 kilometres, and turn right on Somenos Road to return to Government Street.

To continue the circle tour: turn left on Old Cowichan Lake Road, which runs parallel to Highway 18 all the way to Cowichan Lake. Turn left at the stop sign as you reach the village, cross the bridge over the Cowichan River, and follow the main road to stores, cafes, and pubs.

Follow the South Shore Road west from the village of Lake Cowichan, along the lakeside, signposted for Mesachie Lake and Honeymoon Bay. Mesachie Lake is about 6 kilometres along the road. In the early 1940s, timber companies moved their mills from Sahltam to Mesachie Lake, and set up, for the times, a model community. By 1945, almost 400 people lived in homes with electric lights, running water, fenced yards, and garbage collection, or in the separate camps set aside

The Past in the Present:
Lake Cowichan's Kaatza Station Museum

Back in 1913, residents of Cowichan Lake had reason to celebrate: the Esquimalt and Nanaimo Railway had finally come to town. Instead of jolting their bones on the rough road to the coast, people could now ride in comfort.

In those halcyon days when everyone but a few nay-sayers thought logging of the massive trees of the forest could go on forever, Lake Cowichan village looked like a sure bet for prosperity—and the railway could only help. Since loggers first began cutting trees near the lake, they had pushed and poled the logs down the river to the coast, and floated them on to mills at Chemainus and Genoa Bay. But the Cowichan River is rough and full of rapids and rocks that snared the logs, and made the river drive both dangerous and inefficient. The last log drive took place in 1908. Large-scale exploitation of the forest around the lake began two years later. Mills were built on the lakeshore and the railway arrived to carry logs to the coast. Thus began an era when residents believed Lake Cowichan could be the most prosperous town in British Columbia.

Lake Cowichan's Kaatza Station Museum, beside South Shore Road, reminds the visitor of that era, and of the years that preceded it. Housed in the original E&N station built in 1913, the museum takes its name from the Cowichan Indian word for "big lake," the original term for this area.

Between the museum and the road is a display of logging railway engine and stock, including a 1916 wooden boxcar and a wooden caboose. Inside the museum are a re-created mining tunnel and pioneer home, and various displays that show life in Lake Cowichan between 1890 and 1940.

By 1930, a passerby could describe the road from Duncan to Lake Cowichan, once beautiful, as "a scene of wide and indescribable desolation." Loggers and logging camps moved ever westward, seeking uncut forests, until logging operations were closer to Port Renfrew than to Duncan. Though the logging industry is still a mainstay of the area, everyone now knows the trees were not forever.

Retired logging train at the Lake Cowichan museum.

for Chinese or East Indian workers. The town is now home to the Cowichan Lake Forestry Research Centre, established in 1929. The centre came from the realization that forests needed help to grow back. It specialized in silvicultural studies, including those of natural regeneration, seed production, growth, yield and thinning. It is now the area centre for genetic research on Douglas-fir, yellow cedar, red cedar, western hemlock and Sitka spruce. For a guided tour of the walking trails at the station, call 749-6811.

Keep an eye out as you drive through the village for an avenue of trees, some 240 of thirty-three species imported from around the world more than forty years ago.

The back road from Port Renfrew links into the Lake Cowichan area at the flashing amber light in Mesachie Lake. (See Tour 3.)

The road continues west along the lakeshore to Honeymoon Bay, a small logging community of neat homes on neat streets. This name should have some wild, romantic story attached, but the truth is more mundane: a bachelor went off to England to find a bride, but not before a neighbour suggested he bring her back here to live. Did he find a wife? Did they return? No one knows—but the name remains, and someone was taken enough with the idea that they named the trailer park in town Paradise Village.

About 2.5 kilometres past the Honeymoon Bay dryland sort, a road leads right to Gordon Bay Provincial Park. Stop here for campsites, picnicking, swimming, boat launch, visitor activities, and nice wildflowers in April.

Continue on South Shore Road another kilometre to the Honeymoon Bay Wildflower Reserve, on your left. An easy, half-hour stroll takes you through second-growth Douglas-fir. If you look at the sign in the parking lot, you'll have a better chance of recognizing the flowers and other plants that dot the reserve. Even if it's not late April or early May, when the largest concentration of wild pink lilies on the island will be in bloom, the walk still provides a pleasant interlude in shaded second-growth forest.

Just beyond the wildflower reserve, the road becomes gravel. From here on, follow the signs for Carmanah, Bamfield, and other west-coast points. Keep right at the stop sign 500 metres past the reserve, and continue along the lakeshore. Eleven kilometres from the stop sign is Fletcher Challenge's Caycuse campground, one of a number of recreational areas along the lake where you can picnic.

Cowichan Lake, south shore.

Keep a watch out for the vintage gas station just over a kilometre past the Caycuse log sort. About 3.5 kilometres past the sort, you'll see the Caycuse seed orchard; near here, you can take a right turn to "town."

Just after you cross the bridge over Nixon Creek, keep right, still following the signposts for Carmanah and Bamfield. To your right is the Nixon Creek recreational site on the lake. All along the road now, you can look out across the lake, to see mountains reflected in the water.

At the end of the lake, 6 kilometres past the Nixon Creek recreation site, the road divides. If you are headed for Carmanah, Bamfield, or other west-coast points, keep left (see Tour 8). To complete the tour around the lake and back to Duncan, keep right for Youbou.

TimberWest looks after the Heather Campsite on your right 500 metres from the Carmanah turn-off. **Keep right around the end of the lake, and continue along the north shore road.** This is a pleasanter road than the south shore road; while the south road runs through open and not particularly interesting forest, the north road at this end of the lake is narrower, shaded by maple and alder. It offers better views through moss-draped cedars to the lake and more attractive places to stop for a picnic or a break. It parallels the lake at first, then cuts across country to rejoin the lakeshore a kilometre or two farther on, crossing streams that drain down to the lake. You can stop at an official picnic site or pull off to the side of the road and walk down to the lake to sit on the narrow gravel beach under the trees.

The Youbou mill, on the north shore of Cowichan Lake.

Cowichan Lake has long attracted summer visitors who built cabins and cottages along the shore. Some 13 kilometres east of the lake-end, the road enters a popular cottage area, where cabins crowd along the shore. Maple Grove B.C. Forest Service Recreation Site is in the middle of the area.

Beyond the cabins is the Youbou Mill, where log booms toe in against the shore and mill machinery occupies the land. Created from the names of mill manager and president Yount and Bouten, Youbou's name annoyed early residents, who took to calling the mill town Hoo-doo. Youbou is another company town, built around a new, large mill opened in the mid-1920s. The small mill cottages, the mini-mart, the community bulletin board, the combination pub/cafe/gas station, and the store that sells groceries and rents videos create a picture of lakeside small-town life in the long narrow community that stretches between the lakeshore and the hills behind.

If Youbou shows the older, more settled community aspects of Cowichan Lake life, beyond it is a different view: the big new houses of spreading suburbia. The road runs past these developments to the end of the North Arm of the lake. **Turn right about 9 kilometres past Youbou onto Meade Creek Road. Continue past Springs Beach and across the first bridge over Meade Creek, then turn right onto Marble Bay Road, a gravel side road just before the second Meade Creek bridge.** Park near the gate, off the road, and walk the kilometre to the head of trails that circle Bald Mountain. A map of these trails, which branch out from the Marble Bay Scout and Guide Camp, is available from the Cowichan museum or infocentre.

Various trails include Cub Run, forty minutes return, to the top of Old Wolf's Hill for a view over the village and lake; Beaver Walk, an hour return along the lakeshore; Denninger Scout Trail, three hours return, to the saddle of Bald Mountain for views of the lake, returning via the steep Venturer's Challenge and Beaver Walk—or a further forty-five minutes to the top of the mountain. You can return the way you came or, if you have much energy, time (another three hours), and either a map or a good sense of direction, cut down the mountain to Bald Mountain Marine Park and back along the lakeshore to your car.

Return to Meade Creek Road and follow it back out to the north shore road. Follow North Shore Road to the village, then turn left to return to Highway 18. Turn right on the highway and return to the junction with Highway 1, approximately 26 kilometres. A right turn will bring you back to the centre of Duncan.

If, however, you haven't had enough of back roads, you can turn right from Highway 18, 7 kilometres east of Lake Cowichan village, at Skutz Falls Road, and make an immediate left on the Old Lake Cowichan Road. Follow the old road through forests and farm fields, past incurious dogs who laze in driveways, and past moss-draped trees. **Turn right at the stop sign in 16 kilometres, then turn right on Somenos Road to return to Government Street.**

 ## TOUR 8 · COWICHAN LAKE TO CARMANAH, BAMFIELD, AND PORT ALBERNI

Among the most interesting of south island back-road networks, these gravel routes cross from the centre of the island to the west coast. A south fork leads to Carmanah Provincial Park, where some of the largest trees in the world have been saved from logging. En route is Nitinat Lake, an ocean inlet that is windsurfers' mecca. The north fork heads for Bamfield, on the south shore of Barkley Sound, then returns to the centre of the island at Port Alberni.

To drive all these roads and give them their due is much more than a day's journey: Carmanah alone can occupy a full day if you don't want to camp, several days if you do. The trip to Bamfield from Cowichan Lake is an easy day's journey. You could scoot back to Port Alberni, but an overnight stay in Bamfield gives the visitor time to explore across the inlet or to hike along Pachena Bay.

These gravel roads cover the usual range from wide and well graded to narrow, steep, switchbacked or overgrown. Though a passenger car can be used for all of them—with the usual provisos—it's wise to check at Lake Cowichan or Port Alberni for the latest conditions. Be aware that the information you get may not be up to date. Though there are services at a few points along the road, a full tank of gas, food, drink, and emergency supplies are recommended.

This tour is suitable for cars and drivers who welcome the challenges of gravel back-roading. Best spring through fall. You can choose between the dust of dry days and the mud of wet ones, though traffic is not heavy and dust a big problem only on the most-used sections of the roads. Watch for logging traffic at all times. Unless otherwise posted, these roads are open weekdays and weekends, but some see heavy industrial use.

Before You Go

Two good maps help backroaders. The *Guide to Forest Land of Southern Vancouver Island* should be available from the Lake Cowichan Infocentre, at the Kaatza Museum. MacMillan Bloedel's *Recreation and Logging Road Guide to Forest Lands of West Central Vancouver Island, TFL 44* covers most of these routes. For news of road closures, check with MacBlo at 723-9471 or at the Lake Cowichan Infocentre.

✿ ✿ ✿

This route begins at the west end of Cowichan Lake, at a junction where the road to the right leads around the lake to the north shore, and a left turn takes you towards Nitinat, Carmanah, and Bamfield. To reach this point, travel west from Highway 1 north of Duncan on Highway 18 to Cowichan Lake. Continue on the South Shore Road (see Tour 7) to a junction 41 kilometres from the bridge over the Cowichan River, 68.6 kilometres from Highway 1. Roads to Carmanah should be signposted with small blue and white signs that indicate the distance to various points west of Lake Cowichan— though mindless travellers with spray paint may have defaced some of the signs.

Turn left for Bamfield (83 kilometres), Franklin River (35), Nitinat (26), Port Alberni (75), and Carmanah (53). This road gets bumpier after it veers from the lakeshore through second-growth forest and begins to climb up and down the slopes of the island spine.

Two and a half kilometres from the left turn, keep left again; Kissinger Main branches to the right. A swampy area appears on the right, followed soon by a sign indicating Vernon Creek trestle, the decaying remains of what was once a logging railway bridge over Vernon Creek. Built in 1933, the bridge was 24 metres high. Lapsing into railway talk, the sign tells us the bridge contained twenty-two bents with six piles per bent: bents are the horizontal crosspieces on the trestle, piles the vertical timbers that support the bents.

Past the trestle, the road runs through dark/bright forest, where moss glints in the shafts of sunlight that beam through the trees. TimberWest's TFL 46 ends; MacMillan Bloedel's TFL 44 begins.

Approximately 19 kilometres from the junction at the west end of Cowichan Lake, you reach another signposted junction: left for the east side of Nitinat Lake and Carmanah, right for Bamfield and Port Alberni.

To head for Carmanah, turn left. Some 5.6 kilometres from the junction, keep right to reach the Ditidaht visitor's centre, a motel, gas bar, and small store on the Ditidaht Reserve, where you can buy a T-shirt with attractive native design, munch on fried chicken, wash down the dust with a cold drink, or simply shoot the breeze with the locals. Also nearby is a campsite run by the Ditidaht.

The Ditidaht are part of the coastal Nuu-chah-nulth nation. Originally, the Ditidaht lived on the outer coast, in villages as far south as

A small lake beside the road to Bamfield.

Jordan River, north to Clo-oose at the mouth of Nitinat Lake. When freight boat service up the coast ended in the 1960s and a road was built west from Lake Cowichan, they moved to their present location.

Emerge from the Ditidaht Road back onto the main road, here called South Main. On the right ahead is a road to a Forest Service/ MacBlo campsite. Both this and the Ditidaht campsite provide good picnic sites, with views over Nitinat Lake. On a windy day, which most days are, you can sit on shore and watch the windsurfers who long ago discovered the long expanse of water and predictable winds Nitinat Lake provides, and who flock here in the hundreds every year.

Nitinat is not a lake at all, but an almost landlocked saltwater inlet. The 20-kilometre-long inlet narrows at its mouth into a 2.5-kilometre channel ridged by four sills, probably created when long-ago glaciers deposited silt as they retreated. The bar closest to the ocean is covered by just 2 metres of water; three inner sills sit 3 metres below the lowest normal tides.

Mariners must time their entrances and exits at Nitinat Lake by the tides—but even that is of little help. Because the inlet neck is so constricted, water levels change by only 30 centimetres on each ebb and flood, compared to more than 3 metres on nearby shores. Many are the stories of unwary sailors stranded on one of the sills.

You might think this small tidal flow would make the lake brackish, more fresh water than salt. But fresh water flowing in from the Nitinat River occupies only the top 10 metres of the lake, which is as deep as 180 metres.

South Main loops up the north side of the Caycuse River and crosses the river. Immediately after the bridge, keep right onto Rosander Main (South Main wanders off along lakes and rivers eventually to return to Cowichan Lake).

Rosander Main presents the main challenge on the way to Carmanah: a narrow, switchbacked ascent and descent as the road swings away from Nitinat Lake, providing a marvellous view up and down the inlet. The switchback conquered, it's a relatively uneventful trip over roughish gravel through clearcuts to the end of the road, where you can park and hike into Carmanah.

For a day trip that takes you to some of the biggest and most impressive of Carmanah's trees, park at the parking lot and switchback down the first kilometre of well-prepared trail. Then you can choose (though a day trip leaves time for both): turn left to the Three Sisters, three giant

The Battle for Carmanah

For years, it was only a legend. In 1956, or so the story went, timber cruisers had come upon a mighty giant in the forest, a Sitka spruce that dwarfed any found before. But the story could not be confirmed: there was no record of the discovery. And there seemed no hurry to search out this or the other tall Sitka spruce that grew on the rainforest gravel bars of Carmanah Creek. Though the watershed was within the Tree Farm Licence of timber giant MacMillan Bloedel, there were no plans to log this area until 2003.

Then things changed and suddenly, MacMillan Bloedel was in a hurry. When big-tree enthusiast Randy Stoltmann reconnoitred the area in 1988, he found logging roads built and further roads surveyed into the heart of Carmanah, and giant trees marked for cutting the following year.

He and others who valued the west-coast forest could not let this happen. The Sitka spruce of the Carmanah Valley were indeed giants; 90 metres high, 3 metres in diameter, five hundred years old, they were magnificent trees that must be preserved. Within weeks, the Western Canada Wilderness Committee, the Sierra Club and the Heritage Forests Society of British Columbia threw themselves into a campaign to save Carmanah.

The three presented a proposal to add the 6,730-hectare watershed to Pacific Rim National Park. MacBlo responded by halting road construction for a month's study of the area. Volunteers began to build a trail, but it was employees of the forest company who discovered that the legend was true. The Carmanah Giant speared 95 metres into the sky, the tallest known tree in Canada, the tallest Sitka spruce ever recorded anywhere. Just a kilometre from the ocean, it was farther south than

Sitka spruce; turn right to reach Heaven's Grove where Sitka spruce and ferns combine in sunlight and shade.

Return to the Bamfield/Carmanah junction east of Nitinat Lake. To head towards Bamfield if you are coming from Cowichan Lake, turn right. If you are returning from Ditidaht or Carmanah, continue straight on, across the bridge over the Nitinat River. Just past the bridge on the left, a road cuts left, over the Little Nitinat River, signposted to the Nitinat Hatchery and picnic site. Two and a half kilometres down this road is the Nitinat Hatchery, wedged in the Y at the joining of the Little Nitinat and Nitinat rivers.

Beyond the hatchery, the road bumps along the west side of the river, then the lake, narrows, and begins to look increasingly unpromising. The fate of logging roads once logging is completed is to be taken over by anyone seeking it had imagined.

MacMillan Bloedel offered to create reserves of 9 hectares around the Carmanah Giant, and 90 hectares along the creek. But the three environmental groups had already decided they would accept no half measures. If the giant trees were to live, then all the valley must be preserved. Too often, isolated groves of giant trees fall victim to blowdown or to erosion caused by nearby logging. At the mercy of wind, their roots undermined, they crash to the forest floor. The preservationists were determined that this would not happen in Carmanah.

Trail-building crews trekked in to Camp Heaven, by Carmanah Creek. Caravans of people arrived, looked in awe, departed, convinced that the watershed must be protected. The groups produced videos, posters, newspapers, mailers, guides, and maps, making more and more converts to their cause. Artists and writers who went to Carmanah over that summer of 1988 contributed pictures and words to a book, *Carmanah: Artistic Visions of an Ancient Rainforest.*

MacMillan Bloedel tried to bar the trail builders from the TFL land near Carmanah. But the courts said no: a tree farm licence is not ownership. The land was crown land, and anyone could travel on it provided they did not interfere with the TFL holder's exclusive right to log.

A year later, those who wished to preserve Carmanah had both won and lost. Not all the watershed escaped the logger's ax: the upper valley was left outside the park's boundaries. But the Carmanah Giant, the other huge Sitka spruce, and the ancient cedars in the valley were preserved, together with the forests of the surrounding lower valley.

In 1995, the government took the final step, protecting a further 3,400 hectares of the upper Carmanah.

---

scrub brush, with grass growing along the road centre and potholes un-filled. This road is no exception: narrow and rough, marked by bear scat—almost always an indication that few vehicles pass through—it seems a wrong turn, and probably a dead-end.

It is a dead-end, but if you persevere for almost 11 kilometres from the main road, you'll reach the B.C. Forest Service's Knob Point campsite, where canoeists and windsurfers make their base. Quiet and undisturbed by the traffic that uses the road on the east side of the river and lake, it's a nice place to while away an afternoon.

Continue on the road to Bamfield, here called South Main. Far below this road on the left, the Little Nitinat River chatters over rocks. About 6.6 kilometres from the hatchery road, Flora Main departs to the left. If you have a map of the area, you can follow Flora Main to central

South Main and on into Bamfield, but the road is usually closed during working hours, and is narrow and winding to boot.

Continue, instead, along South Main, onto an interesting combination: a lane and a half of pavement and half a lane of gravel. If you meet a logging truck, guess who gets the pavement?

Fifteen kilometres from the hatchery road is Francis Lake, with a campsite and swimming beach; 4 kilometres along, you come to Franklin Camp, one of MacMillan Bloedel's logging yards. Follow the signs left around the camp, then rejoin the paved road as it emerges from the camp. A few hundred metres past **Franklin Camp, turn left for Bamfield (signposted).**

The Bamfield road has its moods. In morning or evening, shadows paint many-hued blue mountains receding into the distance, and oblique light creates an effect strongly three-dimensional. Even though this is second-growth forest, it has had decades to grow, and you can get some faint sense of what this country must have looked like a century ago.

But tackle this road when logging trucks are hustling along or workers are hurrying between Bamfield and Port Alberni, trailing long tails of choking dust behind them, and the mood is decidedly less romantic.

Twelve kilometres from the town, the road crosses, then recrosses the Sarita River, then passes Sarita Lake and its recreation site on the right. In spring and fall, the creeks are full-flowing, in late summer almost dry, and the fireweed shows purple around the stony beds.

About 29 kilometres from the Bamfield turn, the road reaches a T-intersection. Turn right to weave down the hill for a look at Alberni Inlet at Poett Nook or the old logging camp of Sarita. Poett Nook isn't a misspelling: it's named for a Dr. Poett, who lived in San Francisco but dabbled in copper claims along Barkley Sound. Turn left 5 kilometres down this road to visit the Poett Nook marina.

Keep right to head for Sarita. Sarita, it is said, was once the largest logging camp in North America—but then, many claims are made for many places in B.C. Keep right at all the Y-junctions, and you'll reach Alberni Inlet, the long, deep fjord that reaches almost halfway across the island, from Barkley Sound to Port Alberni.

Log booms ride close to shore here, with a boom boat or two at anchor. A pretty road runs to the right, beside the water, with an impromptu campsite and somewhat spiffy biffy.

Return to the Bamfield Road intersection and continue on to-

wards Bamfield, past Frederick and Pachena lakes on your left. **About 63 kilometres from South Main, you'll reach a T-intersection. A left turn will take you to the start of the West Coast Trail.**

Because so many people want to hike the 72-kilometre West Coast Trail, but no one wants to be in a pedestrian traffic jam, would-be hikers must obtain a permit to travel from Bamfield south to Port Renfrew. But if you just want to take a look, making a day hike or two, you can do that provided you sign in at park headquarters. Continue left from the intersection, passing the Pachena Bay Indian reserve on your right, to the end of the road and the parking lot for this part of Pacific Rim National Park.

Sign in at park headquarters, and acquire a map and information. You can make a day hike to the Pachena Point lighthouse, wander along the beaches, and camp and picnic on the beach at Pachena Bay, a fist-shaped inlet from the sea with a pointing finger that becomes the Pachena River.

Return to the Bamfield Road, and follow the signs to Bamfield, a sheltered retreat on the wild west coast of Vancouver Island. The site at the west end of Bamfield was for many years the terminus of the trans-Pacific submarine cable. Once a manned cable station was no longer needed, the buildings became the Bamfield Marine Station, a marine biological research station for five western Canadian universities. You can take a look at displays in the lobby throughout the year; from May

The Bamfield docks.

Bamfield

In the city, night light is normal, nothing to be commented on; only darkness surprises. But here by the side of Bamfield Inlet as the autumn night closes in, it is the pools or pinpricks of light that define the tiny town.

Down by the docks, the lights at the fish-cleaning area are still on, and the voices of two fishermen in check shirts and baseball caps sound out over the water. One has been lucky: he is still talking about the 35-pounder (fishers have no truck with metric) he brought in earlier in the day. The other fisherman is more restrained: his luck was limited to a brace of small coho.

Offshore, the lights are on in the luxury cruisers that slid into harbour an hour ago, putting down anchor rather than bellying up to the dock. Down the inlet now comes a smaller light, slowly growing in the dark, as someone from across the inlet and up the way put-puts his way to town in an outboard-powered runabout. And across the water, in Bamfield West, lights go on in the houses and cabins along the boardwalk that is main street.

An hour later, the dark is deeper, and you can see the stars in the sky: a thousand pinpricks, the flashing red and green lights of a passing plane, the sudden streak of a falling star. That's the measure of the lights in a Bamfield night. No single light, not

through August, you can tour the station Saturday or Sunday between 1 and 3 p.m.

Return along the Bamfield Road to its intersection with Franklin and South Main, and keep straight on at the stop sign, signposted for Port Alberni. The wide, winding, well-graded gravel road, with some

A decaying building on the waterfront at Bamfield.

even the sum of light, washes out the night sky.

Though Bamfield has changed over the years, it still preserves that sense of slow pace and small-town feeling. It is really two towns, the one on the east side of the inlet, attached by gravel road to Port Alberni and the south island, and the one on the west side of the inlet, reachable only by boat. So far, Bamfield has resisted pressures to build a road to link the west town to the east, replying to cries that progress must come by demanding, "Define progress."

On the east side, houses, a motel or two, a store, a pub, a restaurant, marine shops, slowly decaying unoccupied buildings on pilings, crowd near the wharf. Down on that wharf, fishers clean their fish and trade stories, for, despite a declining stock of Pacific salmon, they still home in on Bamfield. And because it is a protected harbour on a coast that has few such harbours, craft from million-dollar yachts down to kayaks paddled by intrepid loners tie up at the wharf.

Across the narrow inlet is the other half of Bamfield, one where vehicles don't intrude and few tourists venture. Bamfield's famed boardwalk—a necessity in wet, west-coast villages—fronts the ocean, with houses, cabins, and the occasional resorts dotted around the peninsula. Across the peninsula is Brady's Beach, sandy strips of beach between rocky headlands where Sitka spruce and shore pine grow.

seal-coating to cut the dust, runs some 45 kilometres into town, mostly along Alberni Inlet. The occasional pull-over on the left side of the road affords views of mountains, valleys, and the inlet.

Just over 30 kilometres along Franklin Main, a road (signposted for traffic coming the other way) cuts left at an acute angle, down into China Creek Park and marina. The steep, curving—but paved— road descends through huge Douglas-firs to a very busy campsite, recreational vehicle site and marina, a favourite spot for Port Alberni residents to launch their boats for a day's fishing, or for other visitors to base camp for fishing forays. You'll find no sign of the people this creek was named for, Chinese immigrant miners who panned for gold here in the 1880s. Stop at the coffee shop for burgers, fries, coffee, and fishing talk.

Return to the main road and continue towards Port Alberni. Sawdust and woodchip piles mark a dryland sort 6 kilometres on; a kilometre and a half later, you're back on pavement. The road continues through a logging camp to a Y-intersection; keep right if you want to explore over to Mount Arrowsmith (and have a map).

Keep left and you'll emerge into the centre of Port Alberni.

CHAPTER 3

The Central Island

AS LONG AS YOU STAY ON THE SOUTHERN TIP OF THE ISLAND OR in the Cowichan Valley, you can fool yourself about the nature of Vancouver Island. But as soon as you venture north of Chemainus, the reality of this mountainous island overwhelms you. The coastal plain narrows and the mountains crowd in from the west. Ladysmith, Nanaimo. Parksville, Qualicum Beach, all lie close up against the ocean, and few back roads connect one to the other.

The main highways in the central island form a sprawling T, with Highways 1 and 19 a coast-hugging crossbar, and Highway 4 the stem that reaches from east coast to west coast, following for the most part lake and river valleys through the mountains. There is little room for meandering back roads either on the narrow coastal plain or in the valleys, and where there is room, people increasingly choose to build their houses. Twenty years ago, the paved back roads that encircle Nanaimo led through farm land and woodland, with open views out over the Strait of Georgia. But Nanaimo has expanded steadily, and now suburban houses flank many of those roads, making them less interesting to backroads drivers.

There are exceptions to this urban sprawl. South of Nanaimo, the roads that criss-cross the Cedar-Yellow Point area are still rural and attractive. The driver weary of highway can still find some interesting alternate routes between Nanaimo and Parksville, and west towards Port Alberni. The Beaver Creek valley northwest of Port Alberni has not succumbed to housing developments.

And gravel logging roads honeycomb the regions west of Nanaimo and west of Port Alberni. Back-roads drivers can find forests, lakes, rivers, and inlets along these unpaved roads.

Resources

The *Guide to Forest Land of Southern Vancouver Island* covers the territory as far north as Qualicum Beach and west to Port Alberni. The *Port Alberni Forest District Recreation Map* published by the B.C. Ministry of Forests gives a general idea of the area. For logging roads around Port Alberni, the best map by far is the *Recreation and Logging Road Guide to the Forest Lands of West Central Vancouver Island* published by MacMillan Bloedel.

TOUR 9 NANAIMO AND SOUTH

Fortunately for backroaders, the area south and west of Nanaimo has not attracted the same attention as waterfront areas north of the city. Back roads remain rural, and logging roads still cut through untenanted forest. This tour leaves Nanaimo through the Harewood Valley at the west side of the city, curls along the edge of the mountains and strikes into the Nanaimo Lakes region. It returns east, crosses the highway, and explores the Yellow Point/ Cedar area before heading back north to Nanaimo.

The tour can take a few hours or a full day, depending on how much exploring you want to do in the Nanaimo Lakes region and how many stops you make en route.

This is an all-season route, though logging roads in the Nanaimo Lakes area should be avoided in snowy weather. Most of the roads are paved and suitable for cyclists and all vehicles, again with the exception of the Nanaimo Lakes logging roads. Note that the Nanaimo Lakes logging roads beyond Second Lake are open only on weekends and evenings. Construction of the new Island Highway bypass around Nanaimo may mean some detours.

The tour includes pleasant walks through forested parks, rushing rivers (though not in summer), tranquil lakes, good views of mountain and sea, seaside beaches, farm stands, pubs, and cafes.

Before You Go

A general map of the Nanaimo area, such as that available at local tourist infocentres, is a good reference. Unfortunately, all of the maps of the Nanaimo Lakes region issued by the Ministry of Forests and various logging companies are inaccurate and misleading, as is the map on the sign near the start of those roads. If you are planning to explore this area, take food, drink, and the usual emergency supplies with you, and be prepared to ask fellow backroaders, especially those in pickup trucks, where each road leads.

⚙ ⚙ ⚙

The tour begins in Nanaimo, southbound from the centre of town along the long-time Island Highway, here called Nicol Street. Turn right (west) onto Milton Street at the traffic lights. About .7 kilometres along, turn left on Albert Street, and follow the road as it curves down the hill and becomes Fourth Street. You are now in the Harewood Valley, a dip between the ridge that slopes down to the city seafront and the mountains that wedge the city in from the west.

About .8 kilometres along, turn left onto Harewood Road, and just over a kilometre later, turn left at the sign for Colliery Dam Park. About the only evidence remaining of Nanaimo's colonial past as a coal-mining town appears in museum displays, gravestones, miners' cottages, and some area names. The lakes in this 27.5-hectare park were created by damming the Chase River, to provide a water supply for #1 mine on the Nanaimo waterfront. You can stroll through the woods here, particularly pleasant in fall, and along the stream and lakes.

Return to Harewood Road, which now becomes Nanaimo Lakes Road, and continue west. The road passes Department of National Defence property, then crosses the new island highway that cuts inland from the ocean behind Nanaimo. **Just past the new highway, turn right into the Morrell Nature Sanctuary.**

Trails that range from 700 metres to several kilometres long crisscross this wooded area, best known for the native plants that have been preserved in this sanctuary. Rocky Knoll Trail, Beaver Pond Trail, and trails to the lake or through the forest of cedar, alder, maple, and Douglas-fir all have their own attractions.

Return to Nanaimo Lakes Road and continue southwest. In years past, adventurous backroaders could make a right turn a few hundred metres along, and navigate the narrow, twisting road to the top of Mount Benson. But that road is now closed by gates; and if you want to reach the mountain top, you can make a long hike. The road then crosses a dam and continues past small fields and a few houses, into second-growth forest of cedar, Douglas-fir, and alder, with the mountains coming into view ahead.

About 10 kilometres past the new highway, turn right at the stop sign onto Nanaimo River Road, to drive through areas that have been cut and replanted over the years. Rough roads and tracks that cut off to the left lead to favourite spots along the Nanaimo River, which can be glimpsed far below through power line cuts.

Continue along Nanaimo River Road into TimberWest Coast Wood Supply Division. About 10 kilometres from Nanaimo Lakes Road, keep an eye open on your right for a beaver pond; you can park at a small pull-off just beyond and take a look at beaver dams at the pond's outlet.

The Deadwood Creek campground and picnic area is on your left about 11 kilometres from Nanaimo Lakes Road. Just beyond is a TimberWest security gate, where you must buy a sticker for two dollars and register your vehicle. You may be able to pick up a photocopied map of the Nanaimo Lakes area from the gatekeeper, but bear in mind that this will give you only a general idea of the area, since many of the roads marked on the map are now closed. Just past the gate is the access road to the Deadwood Creek campground.

Most who want to explore this area use dirt bikes, small ATVs, or shank's mare to travel unmaintained roads where gates now bar vehicle traffic. Such travel can be rewarding: one frequent visitor described how to reach the beaver ponds up behind the power line, and noted that the bear up there wasn't dangerous, since she didn't have cubs this year, and revealed that the wolf has cubs, but she won't bother you either.

About 5 kilometres from the gate, the road passes a dryland sort on the right, then the TimberWest offices on the left. Optional: half a kilometre past the office, turn left for the First Lake campsite, at the end of the lake, where you can picnic as you watch fly fishers and canoeists on the lake and the Nanaimo River. On the main road, just under a kilometre past this turn, is Stop 1 on the Nanaimo Lakes elk habitat tour. The BC Forest Service and TimberWest publish a brochure detailing this self-guided tour, but the brochure is out of print, and many of the signs are half-hidden behind tangles of brush. And that's a shame, because a lot of work went into this effort, and few now have access to the information.

Continue on past Second Lake, where elderly cabins crowd in along the shore, and men in baseball caps discuss engines as they peer into the depths of pickup trucks and Jeeps. **Midway along Second Lake, past steep rock faces that shelve down to the water, is a gate that bars access past this point during working hours.** Beyond the end of the lake, a road heads right, up to Echo and Panther Lake; you can try this

Elk, Deer, and the Nanaimo Lakes Region

About 150 of Vancouver Island's 3,000 Roosevelt elk live in the Nanaimo Lakes region. Both the elk and the black-tailed deer that share habitat with them require sufficient forage, good water, and cover that hides them from predators—animal and human. This cover protects them from excessive heat and cold, and, because snow is not as deep below trees or brush, allows them to feed in winter.

Deer and elk range through the Nanaimo Lakes area, from higher elevations in summer to low elevations in winter. The stops on the tour show some features of elk habitat.

Stop 1 marks partially screened wetland, a bog where grasses and sedge that provide a food supply throughout the year grow. Some bushes and trees provide a partial screen between the road and the bog.

Stop 2, near the end of Second Lake, shows interspersion of forage and cover. Douglas-firs that sprouted after a 1900 fire provide cover; nearby, along a short path, is heavy undergrowth that provides excellent foraging.

Stop 3, close to Stop 2, shows a forty-year-old forest, with a stand of deciduous trees and undergrowth that provides good habitat for both elk and deer.

At Stop 4, across Rush Creek, you must climb the bank behind the sign to see hidden wetland favoured by elk.

Stop 5, beside a small lake on the road that leads up Rush Creek towards Panther Lake, shows elk winter range, with abundant grasses, sedge, and deer fern along the lakeshore.

Stop 6 is beside a stand of trees planted in 1958, spaced in 1979, and fertilized in 1980. Because logging slash was not removed from some of this area, few forage plants grow and elk cannot move easily through the area.

Stop 7 points out a stand of conifers clear-cut in 1960 and replanted in 1962. Unthinned, it allows little light through the forest canopy; as a result, not much vegetation grows on the forest floor.

Stop 8 shows an area clear-cut in 1989. You can look from this viewpoint across the river to see a meadow where clumps of trees provide good cover, and open areas provide good forage.

The Nanaimo River west of Second Lake.

route, but it may or may not be possible for two-wheel-drive vehicles.

A few hundred metres past the Panther Lake turn is Elk Tour Stop 2.

Just under 5 kilometres from the Echo/Panther Lake turn, the road straight ahead crosses a bridge over the Nanaimo River; a row of stones painted orange and red just before the bridge makes this junction unmistakeable. This is where the maps are most misleading, since they show roads now closed. These roads do change, so be prepared to make judgements: you may have to turn around and retreat or risk losing a muffler or denting an undercarriage.

Optional: you can turn right before the bridge to briefly follow the Nanaimo River, then Rush Creek. Cross a creek—beware of the bumpy bridge—and keep left, to pass Stop 5 on the elk habitat tour. The road, narrow, potholed, and a little overgrown, runs along the river again, overarched with maples and alder, lined with cedar. Watch for culverts where the road has sunk, leaving a sudden dip in the surface.

You can go as far as you wish and your car can handle on this road; a turn 5.6 kilometres from the Nanaimo River bridge will take you up Tangle Mountain, but this road is passable only by four-wheel-drive, high-clearance vehicles. The river road is increasingly difficult, and it's probably best to turn around—but even with a retreat, the road is worthwhile, affording pleasant views over the river and lake, and possible picnic sites along the way.

The road straight on across the Nanaimo River bridge leads to Fourth Lake, and a tangle of roads to various creeks, elk grazing areas, and the defunct Green Mountain ski area. Follow the main road through all turns for the next few kilometres. Three kilometres from the Nanaimo River bridge, a road leads left towards Green Mountain. The main Nanaimo Lakes Road continues west, along the river, and past elk tour stop 6 and 7. **Just .6 kilometres past tour stop 7, a minor road departs through the brush to the left.** The sign noting that this road leads to Fourth Lake was falling down and may be gone by now.

Bear left onto this road. It's rough, narrow, and steep, so must be driven at low speed; keep an eye out for potholes or drop-offs. Half a kilometre along is a Y in the road. If you stop and walk along the right-hand fork of the Y, you'll reach the spillway from the dam that contains Fourth Lake. In winter, it forms a marvellous and noisy cascade, one of the main sources for the Nanaimo River.

The left fork of the Y leads to the dam and the lakeshore. The road is rough and rocky here, so you might prefer to park and walk in.

Return to the main road, trek back past Second Lake and the security gate, and retrace your route along Nanaimo River Road. Seventeen and a half kilometres along, turn left onto White Rapids Road, then turn left onto Godfrey Road.

From the 1860s to the 1950s, Nanaimo was a coal town, much of its prosperity based on the coal mines that underlay its harbour, and fringed it to north and south. The first coal mines worked were near the waterfront in the centre of present-day Nanaimo; the next set of shafts were dug to the north, at Wellington. When coal was discovered south of the town, the new mines were named Wellington Extension—which became Extension—so that people would associate Extension's coal with the good reputation earned by the Wellington seam.

The Extension mines, however, lay more than 8 kilometres from Wellington. Drive into the town of Extension, past the old cottages and new trailers, new homes and old fences, and you will see faint signs of those mines, the last of which closed in the 1930s. Continue straight on into town, then turn right on Baker Street, and right again—or park by the side of the road and follow the old tracks to see piles of old tailings, now well grown over.

Continue straight on at the stop sign, having driven three sides of a square through Extension, then keep left on Extension Road. You have to look hard, but coal dust, tailings, and the remains of old timbering still lie in the underbrush.

Extension Road takes you back out to White Rapids Road. **Turn right, and drive through the Cinnabar Valley back to Nanaimo River Road. Turn left on Nanaimo River Road, and follow it down to the highway. Turn right onto Highway 1 south. Move into the left lane; you'll pass the Cassidy Inn on your left, Cassidy Road on your right, and cross a green bridge. Immediately after the bridge, make a cautious left turn (there is a left turn lane) onto Haslam Road.**

By crossing the highway, you have moved from a region of old mines and logging into a gentle country of farms and woods. The road skirts the back of the Nanaimo Airport—watch for gliders, whose pilots find the air currents here superb for their sport—and **keep right 1.4 kilometres from the highway onto Adshead Road,** which runs past farm fields, barns, horses, Holstein cattle, and a herb farm to Cedar Road. Harold Adshead ranks a mention in local histories; a well-liked butcher, he gave wieners to children who came shopping with their parents.

Turn left on Cedar Road. Cedar is one of four euphoniously named districts north of Ladysmith: Bright, Oyster, Cranberry, and Cedar. Bright was so-named, or so it is said, because from it you could see the lights on ships in Chemainus Harbour; Cranberry for its swamp cranberries; oyster for the small native oysters that seeded there; and Cedar, of course, for the groves of cedar trees thereabouts. It's nice to know that Bright, Oyster, Cranberry and Cedar weren't four officers on a Royal Navy ship.

The first farmers settled in Cedar in the 1860s, brought along the coast and up the rivers by helpful Sney-ny-mo Indians. In the papers of these settlers, there is much mention of squared logs, oxen and pigs, commodities not much in evidence today. You're more likely to see dairy cattle and roadside stands for brown eggs and ordinary and exotic vegetables.

A kilometre and a half from the Adshead/Cedar roads intersection, turn right to Yellow Point on Yellow Point Road. Follow Yellow Point Road through gently undulating farm country, past an equestrian centre and a home business that specializes in porcelain dolls, to yellow Point Park, a small wedge of land with trails through arbutus and grass. About 2 kilometres past the park, a driveway on the right leads to Yellow Point Lodge.

Yellow Point Lodge fulfilled a dream for Gerry Hill, who first saw the seaside property in 1911 when he was sailing. Eleven years later, he bought the land, but it was another eight years before he could move here from Vancouver with his wife and children. In 1935, he opened a resort: small, rustic cabins, and a dining room in the family cabin. Hill opened the big log lodge in 1939; it prospered and became a favourite holiday destination for generations of Vancouverites and Victorians.

Sadly, the present building is no longer the original Yellow Point Lodge. That building burned in 1985. The 1986 replacement, together with many of the original cabins, are still crowded every year with people who have been coming here for many years. Hill died in 1988, at the age of ninety-four; his son runs the resort.

In 1914, it still took three hours to go from Yellow Point to Nanaimo. If you want, it can now take you twenty minutes, but a backroader can still easily spend three hours. Just beyond Yellow Point Lodge is Blue Heron Park on the right, with picnic tables and a path that leads down to a pebble beach good for wandering. Just under 3 kilometres past the lodge, Roberts Memorial Provincial Park is on the right. This 14-hectare park was donated to the people of B.C. by resident May Vaughan Roberts, in memory of her husband and daughter. Walk down to the sandstone

The Crow and Gate Pub near Cedar.

beach and look out over the sea; in March and April, sea lions gather near the shore.

Just under 6 kilometres from the park entrance is another reason not to hurry back to Nanaimo, looking neither left nor right. To the left here is the Crow and Gate Pub, a local fixture since 1972 and one of the first neighbourhood pubs in British Columbia. Many a new building meant to look traditional ends up simply looking fraudulent, but the long, low Crow looks just right. It's modelled after a pub in Sussex, England. Inside, the huge fireplace—big enough to roast an ox if Cedar still had any—and the long tables create a good country pub atmosphere.

Half a kilometre up the road, **bear right onto Cedar Road.** St. Philip's Anglican Church, on the left 1.6 kilometres from the junction, has a long history: the first church, opened in 1892, burned down in 1907; this church dates from 1908. If the church is open, take a look at the rood screen, built by the Royal Engineers for St. Paul's Esquimalt and moved here in 1936.

The small, strung-out community of Cedar still has a fine rural flavour, enhanced by the local businesses and small houses on either side of the road. The Wheatsheaf Inn, on the right as you approach town, is partly new construction, but the old inn still survives. The first hotel here was built in 1882, and served as a stagecoach stop. That building burned in 1926. Nothing daunted, the owner immediately bought two nearby houses, towed them by horsepower to this spot, and joined them together to form his new inn.

At the north end of Cedar, the road comes to a T-intersection. **Turn right if you want to visit the Harmac pulp mill, left if you want to return to Nanaimo.** Harmac offers mill tours, and you may see, hear, and possibly smell sea lions that hang out on the booms and make life difficult for mill employees and other harbour denizens.

To reach Nanaimo, cross the Nanaimo River and continue along Cedar Road. The road will meet the Island Highway about 3 kilometres along; bear right towards the city. About 1.4 kilometres north, turn right on Haliburton Road.

Most people entering the city from the south will miss this road, which provides the best views of the bay and the city's harbour. The ground slopes steeply down to the water, where log booms and boom boats abound.

Haliburton goes through old Nanaimo, flanked by some new houses and many of the old cottages built while the mines were still active. **When you reach Milton Street, turn left to return to the tour starting point, or continue straight on to reach downtown Nanaimo.**

TOUR 10: NANAIMO AND NORTH

As Nanaimo's suburbs spread north, it's ever harder to find attractive back roads. Where once the view was of water glimpsed through sturdy native trees, now it's more likely to be of peach stucco houses with double gables, stolidly occupying treeless lots. But a few back roads still exist, alternatives to the highway on the road north. This section outlines several such roads that you can patchwork together to spend minimum time on the highway as you head north.

None of the tours are lengthy; with the exception of the Horne Lake route, each is suitable for a quiet hour or two away from the busy highway.

All except the Horne Lake road are paved, suitable for any vehicle and driver. They include occasional seafront views, pubs and cafes, walks through small parks, garden produce from stands, and craft markets.

They're good for cyclists—perhaps the only routes much fun for cyclists who want to head north from Nanaimo.

Before You Go

I've yet to find an accurate map that covers this area properly. On the other hand, you won't need maps for most of the area, since choices are few and, for the most part, logical. One pamphlet well worth getting in advance is *Snags, seedlings, and salamanders: a self-guided tour of the Horne Forest Service Road*, available from the Port Alberni Forest District, 4227 Sixth Avenue, Port Alberni, B.C. V9Y 4N1; telephone 724-9205.

✤ ✤ ✤

I *Jingle Pot Road, Nanaimo*

The first alternate route north takes you from the centre of Nanaimo to the highway just north of town. **Start by turning west on Comox Road at its junction with old Highway 1 (not the new bypass) near the centre of Nanaimo. Follow Comox Road past Bowen Park on the right,** stopping for a wander through the woods and along the Millstream. That this road is named Comox tells you something about the progression of road-building in the area: Comox is part of the old Island Highway, replaced by the newer highway to the northeast, which is being replaced in its turn by a newer island highway that bypasses Nanaimo to the west.

Comox Road becomes Bowen Road. Continue to the traffic lights at Wakesiah Road, and turn left. Turn right on Jingle Pot Road. Jingle Pot's name dates back to coal-mining days, when coal was sent down to the waterfront from the mines in pots that ran on an overhead cable.

Just under 2 kilometres along, Jingle Pot passes the Buttertubs Marsh on the right. You can park just past the marsh and walk the chip trail around this wildlife sanctuary. The road continues west then north through an area that is increasingly built up, passing on the left Westwood Road, which leads to Westwood Lake Park, a favourite summer refuge for generations of Nanaimo kids.

Leaving the town behind, Jingle Pot runs between farm fields and through Douglas-fir and cedar second growth for about 10 kilometres. There will be an interchange where Jingle Pot crosses the new Nanaimo Parkway portion of the Island Highway so you can head north on this new road, or continue to the old Island Highway on Mostar Road, and turn north again.

II Lantzville Road

Approximately 5 kilometres north of Nanaimo, the Lantzville Road veers right, towards the water and the village of Lantzville. Follow the road through the village—pub, cafe, small stores, view of the water—and continue along until it rejoins the island highway 5 kilometres from the first turn-off. This is a pleasant drive through a community sprawled along the seafront. Lantzville was named for one of the money men behind a nearby coal mine. In its early years, the settlement was made up mainly of small miners' houses. When the mines closed, the houses were rented out to people who were looking for a quiet home in the country—the beginning of the Lantzville tradition. Eventually, those houses were sold and moved so the land could be subdivided and new houses built.

The Lantzville Hotel opened in 1924, and was run by the same owner into the 1960s. In that decade, the owner confided to a newspaper reporter that he would like to be able to sell wine as well as cider and beer, for cider after all was a type of wine, and he could not see the difference. But he drew the line at dancing. "No dancing," he was reported as saying, "no dancing at all. Dancing might cause trouble, and most people out for a glass of beer or wine won't want trouble."

III Northwest Bay Road

The Island Highway continues north to parallel Nanoose Harbour. **Past this bay, at the traffic lights, turn right onto Northwest Bay Road.** Northwest Bay Road curls across the flats at the head of Nanoose Harbour; keep an eye out for eagles that cluster here in early winter. Cross the railway tracks, **then turn right just over a kilometre from the highway onto Powder Point Road.** Cross the tracks again, then continue straight on at the stop sign into Fairwinds, a community planned around a golf course.

To the right, 4 kilometres from the beginning of Powder Point Road, is the entrance to Canadian Forces Experimental and Test Ranges. For many years, protestors have gathered across Nanoose Harbour from this base, protesting against American nuclear submarines that use the test range here.

The road runs through the Fairwinds community, cutting across the golf course and past new homes clustered along the course and on winding side roads, then passes older, smaller houses along the waterfront and the Schooner Cove Resort hotel and marina on the right. **Continue to a stop sign at Northwest Bay Road, and turn right.**

A real estate sign and a small cabin send conflicting messages about waterfront off Claudet Road, near Northwest Bay.

A few hundred metres along this road, turn right again onto Claudet Road. Claudet passes through arbutus groves and Douglas-fir and cedar to a marina and a small community of modest homes. About 4 kilometres from Northwest Bay Road are a rustic sign and parking area for Beachcomber Park, where you can follow a trail through the woods to a small and pleasant cove, a good place for a picnic or a little beach-walking.

Continue on Claudet; it curves back on itself and returns to Northwest Bay Road. Turn right on Northwest Bay Road. A left in a kilometre and a half will take you to the Rocking Horse Pub; otherwise, continue north to return to the Island Highway 5.6 kilometres farther on. On your left as you rejoin the highway is Craig Heritage Park and a travel infocentre. The park contains heritage buildings from the Parksville area; these include an 1886 post office, an 1885 log house, and a 1912 church.

IV Errington to Qualicum

This route begins at the centre of Parksville, where Highway 4 leads towards Port Alberni and the west coast. **Turn west with Highway 4. Just over 5 kilometres from this junction, turn left at the turn signposted for Errington and Englishman River Falls.**

This route provides good views of the island's mountain spine rising from a foreground of dairy farms and forest. Just over 5 kilometres from the highway is a stop sign, at the centre of the village of Errington.

Errington doesn't have a notably romantic past, yet an early resident must have found it romantic enough. Duncan McMillan is thought to have named the village where he settled after Errington, in Northumberland, which plays a role in Sir Walter Scott's poem *Jock of Hazeldean*. Northumberland's Errington saw action in the border wars; Vancouver Island's Errington is peaceable, with more of a reputation for the craft and produce market that takes place Saturday mornings, or for the alternative culture that has taken solid root: the variety store sells brown eggs and auto accessories, but also special bottled water.

Continue straight on about 7 kilometres to reach Englishman River Falls Provincial Park, as nice an oasis as you'll find on a hot summer's day. The river, said to be named for an Englishman who drowned here in the 1880s, has gouged a deep cleft in the rock, and the falls tumble over into the gorge. Douglas-fir, cedar, and ferns create a dark cool forest; trails cut through the forest and follow the river. This is a popular campsite, almost always full on summer weekends.

Return to the junction at the centre of Errington. Turn left (west) onto Grafton Road. This area behind Coombs and the highway west to Port Alberni is home to many a small farmer and craftsperson. Along the

An old farm tractor on the roads south of Highway 4.

road are farms and farm stands, ostentatious peach stucco outgunned by more eclectic weathered wood and clapboard, and small businesses that might sell guns and powder or equally well pottery and weavings. Continue past a blueberry farm (stop in summer for fine berries and fresh vegetables) to a crossroad about 7 kilometres from the Errington junction where the road straight ahead is marked as a no-through road. **Turn right onto Pratt Road.**

Pratt cuts through more farm fields and woods, past small businesses and farms, then on the right a machinery yard that has elevated rust to an art form. **Just beyond, turn left at Highway 4.** (If you want to visit the village of Coombs, famed for the goats that nibble the grass on the market roof and for a dozen or so souvenir shops and stores, turn right.)

Continue west on Highway 4. About a kilometre west, turn right, onto the road signposted for Qualicum Beach.

This cut-off, known as Highway 4A, is surprisingly little used. It passes through rural country; you may want to make a stop at the Wooden Nickel, a huge antique market .7 kilometres from the highway, at the railway whistle stop of Hilliers. About 4 kilometres from Highway 4 is an interchange with the new Island Highway, scheduled for completion in 1996; you can head north or south here. Otherwise, follow 4A down into the village of Qualicum Beach. **Follow the road to a stop sign, then turn left on Memorial Avenue to return to the waterfront version of Highway 1.**

V Horne Lake Back Roads

Many island travellers have driven the Horne Forest Service Road as far as Horne Lake and the Horne Lake caves. Few have followed it on along the Qualicum River, across a minor height of land to Rosewall Creek, then back across country to the coast. The road beyond Horne Lake is now being upgraded; running through mature second-growth timber, it is one of the most attractive forestry roads on the south island.

You'll enjoy it much more if you obtain a copy of the pamphlet describing a self-guided tour, available from the Port Alberni Forest District Office. Just in case you didn't think that far ahead, some of the following information is drawn from that pamphlet. **A word of warning: until the upgrading is complete, some stretches of the road are paved with large, sharp gravel, and drivers should drive slowly and with caution.**

Fourteen kilometres north of Qualicum Beach, turn left onto

Horne Lake Road at the Horne Lake store. Half a kilometre later, turn right at a T-intersection, again signposted for Horne Lake. The road crosses the new Island Highway; the next three lefts are signposted to Spider Lake. **Continue straight on to Horne Lake, following the directions on small blue and white signs along the road.** Arbutus and small Douglas-fir overhang the road as you approach the lake. **Keep left 10 kilometres from the highway; the lake soon appears on your left.**

The road runs through a tunnel of trees, between the cliffs that climb to the mountains on your right and small cabins clustered on the shore to your left. Wherever there is a small flat space by the lake, someone has built a cabin, for year-rounders or summer residents, in little colonies along the shore.

At the end of the lake on the left is a private campground where you can get information on and equipment for the Horne Lake caves. Just beyond is the parking lot for Horne Lake Caves Provincial Park. A 400-metre trail leads from the parking lot across a swinging suspension bridge over the Qualicum River to the main cave; other trails lead on to three more caves that are open to the public. You can arrange for cave tours by calling the number listed on the notice board at the start of the trail.

Like most of the 1,000 known caves on Vancouver Island, these caves are hollowed out of limestone. Limestone is formed from the skeletons of marine organisms deposited on ancient seabeds aeons ago; acidic water dripping onto the limestone dissolves part of it and eventually forms caves.

Return to Horne Lake Road and continue west. This Forest Service road follows the Qualicum River northwest toward its source, a pleasant drive along the stream. From this point on, you'll see numbered signs that point out stops on the self-guided tour. Some of the most interesting are listed below:

Stop 4 (4.0 kilometres from the park entrance): a trail parallels the river here, passing a small waterfall and the remnants of a 1930s logging railway trestle.

Stop 6 (9.0 kilometres): in this area are stumps that remain from hand logging in the 1930s. Look for springboard notches near the bases of these stumps. Since pockets of pitch, twisted wood grain, and butt swell made it difficult and unprofitable to cut the tree near its base, loggers cut notches and hammered in springboards on which they stood to wield their axes higher up.

The Qualicum River near Horne Lake caves

Stop 7 (12.0 kilometres): from the summit, waters flow southeast to feed the Qualicum River, northwest to feed Rosewall Creek. If clouds and fog don't obscure the view, you can see bare snags, evidence of a large 1930s forest fire caused by man.

Stop 8 (13.0 kilometres): a short trail leads to a bog; look for beavers and their dam that has created a pond.

Stop 9 (15.0 kilometres): look for remains of the log skids, firebox, and boiler of a steam donkey used in logging several decades ago.

Stop 10 (16.0 kilometres): this area was clear-cut in 1929, slash-burned in 1930, and replanted with Douglas-fir. The trees were spaced when they were about forty years old, fertilized in 1979.

Stop 14 (25.0 kilometres): follow a short trail to a viewpoint that looks out over the east coast and the Strait of Georgia.

Stop 15 (25.0 kilometres): a nearby trail leads to what remains of three logging railway trestles built in the 1930s. The Ministry of Forests warns: these trestles are unsafe; please keep off.

This road, like many others through forested areas, varies with the seasons. In winter, the creeks and rivers swell with the rain and rush head-long over gravel beds and down chutes. The clouds crowd in, and mist hangs in the tree tops. But in summer, the creeks dwindle, the sun burns through the tree tops, and the forest grows dry and dangerously suscepti-ble to fire.

Past the 25-kilometre point, the road descends a long hill, curves and approaches the new island highway. **At the interchange here, you can turn north for Courtenay or south for Qualicum, or you can continue to the old Island Highway and the seaside communities of Deep Bay and Fanny Bay.** The road emerges onto the coastal highway just south of a sign marking Cook Creek—a sign that would probably send 1930s gazetteer writers into gentlemanly fits of fury. "Chef Creek," reads that old gazetteer, "**not** Cook Creek." By the 1950s, the hard line had softened a little: "Chef (Cook) Creek." And the Ministry of Highways has found one way of settling what seems to have been a bitter dispute, as these things go: on its map showing the route of the new highway, it names one area creek "Cook," its neighbour "Chef." Once back on the coastal highway, you can consider such monumental questions over a beer and a feed of oysters at the Fanny Bay Inn.

 **PORT ALBERNI WEST**

Backroaders have been driving the logging roads northwest of Port Alberni for decades, drawn by the scenery, the possibilities for exploring, and the fishing in a scatter of small lakes. This tour leads you from Port Alberni west then north, through provincial parks, along lakesides and rivers with distant views of mountains, along narrow and disused gravel roads, then back through farm country to attractive waterfalls and a heritage sawmill. Allow half a day for the trip; take with you food and drink, plus the usual emergency supplies standard for logging back roads.

Suitable for drivers who like gravel roads and who aren't averse to the occasional stretch of overgrown, narrow track that demands slow speeds and some faith in the road ahead. Not suitable for large RVs, for bicycles, or for drivers for whom losing a muffler would be a disaster.

Along the route are lakes, rivers, waterfalls; certain sightings of bear scat and possible sightings of bears; pretty country with good views interspersed with heavy forest. This route links up with the logging roads that tie the Alberni Valley to the Comox Valley.

Best in spring, summer, fall. Check locally for logging traffic; these roads may be closed on weekdays if traffic is heavy.

Before You Go

Pick up a copy of MacMillan Bloedel's *Recreation and Logging Road Guide to the Forest Lands of West Central Vancouver Island: Tree Farm Licence 44* from MacMillan Bloedel offices or from the Port Alberni Forest Information Centre, on Alberni Quay in downtown Port Alberni. The B.C. Forest Ministry's *Port Alberni Forest District Recreation Map* is also useful, though not as accurate or detailed as MacBlo's map. Check with MacMillan Bloedel at 724-5721 or their Sproat Lake division at 724-4433 for traffic reports and road closures.

Warning: the road that follows the north side of Elsie Lake is no longer used by logging traffic. The road is narrow and rutted and the bridge across one of the creeks is deteriorating. Check before you go with the locals—but be aware that it's hard to find anyone who has up-to-date information on conditions here. You may have to turn back, or make a shorter circle.

ॐ ॐ ॐ

Though this is a circle tour that can be driven in either direction, it is slightly easier to find roads and turns if you go in a clockwise direction, beginning at the bottom of Johnston Road (Highway 4) in Port Alberni, where the highway turns right to follow the Somass River on the way towards Tofino.

Follow Highway 4 along the river and across the bridge. About 6.3 kilometres from the Johnston Road junction, on the Tseshaht Reserve, you'll pass the Tseshaht Market, with its Indian craft store.

The Tseshaht, part of the Nuu-chah-nulth nation, moved into this territory in the eighteenth century. Until then, it is thought they lived on the shores of Barkley Sound.

But the sound had no good salmon rivers not already claimed by other groups, and the Tseshaht made their way up Alberni Inlet to establish winter villages near the mouth of the Somass River, where masses of salmon fought their way upstream each fall to spawn. Each fall, the Tseshaht canoed up the inlet, stopping at camps along the way, then settled in for another season at the inlet's end. They established their main village on land now occupied by the pulp mill.

In 1862, Captain Edward Stamp arrived to build a sawmill, and was somewhat annoyed to discover the Tseshaht had no desire to vacate their land. He ordered the captains of two ships to turn their guns on the village, declaring he would destroy all houses. The Tseshaht moved to the banks of the Somass—but were probably made considerably happier when Stamp's mill failed several years later and almost all the white interlopers left.

Four kilometres past the Tseshaht market, turn right to Sproat

Lake Provincial Park on Great Central Lake Road. **Continue straight on (don't turn left to the park)** through fir and cedar second growth and past a few houses. Just under 7 kilometres from the highway, you'll pass the Robertson Creek salmonid enhancement facility (otherwise known as a fish hatchery), where 900,000 juvenile chinook salmon, a million juvenile coho and a quarter-million steelhead trout are produced each year, mainly to replenish the Alberni Inlet pink salmon, coho, and steelhead. You can see juvenile steelhead and coho year-round, chinook in April and May, adult coho and chinook September through November, and spawning steelhead in February. The creek is a tributary of the Somass River, for centuries a major spawning river for salmon and now revitalized by fish from the hatchery.

A kilometre past the hatchery, make an acute right at the Ark Resort, onto gravel Ash Main. The resort, on Great Central Lake, includes a marina and boat launch, and is the main jumping-off point for travellers who want to see 440-metre Della Falls, Canada's highest waterfall, reachable by means of a long boat ride followed by a 16-kilometre trek along Drinkwater Creek. The Ark was originally a floating resort, built in 1912 by settler Joe Drinkwater, the first white man to record seeing Della Falls, which he named for his wife. At the time, Drinkwater was hiking cross-country to win a bet that he could cross Vancouver Island from Bedwell Sound, on the west coast. Though today the resort accepts only campers and RVS, in its heyday the sixteen-bedroom float house welcomed hunters and fishers from around the world.

Head north with Ash Main, through forest and past ubiquitous Stellar's jays; black bears are not uncommon in this area. Seven kilometres from the Ark, keep right; the road to your left dead-ends at Great Central Lake, or hooks up with four-wheel drive roads to the west. **Some 13.7 kilometres from the Ark, a pull-off to the left of the road allows you to park and take a look at the Ash River from the bridge.**

Two kilometres farther on, you'll reach another bridge across the river. Take a moment to look at the view to the west while you consider your options. Ahead to the left is a scenic route that edges above several lakes then twists back to follow the north shore of Elsie Lake. However, it includes a section—along this north shore—that is no longer used by logging companies, and that is therefore falling into disrepair. It includes a bridge that may or may not be passable, and you may have to turn back.

If you decide not to try this section of the route, turn right

The view along Ash Main.

before the river, and keep right at subsequent intersections to rejoin the road that leads to Beaver Creek Road.

If you decide to proceed to Elsie Lake, keep left across the river. About .7 kilometres ahead, keep right on Ash Main. Ash Main, narrow and winding from this point on, demands attentive driving: logging trucks—including off-roaders almost as wide as the road—can come barrelling down from the hills, and you'll have to tuck in to infrequent pull-outs. If this doesn't appeal, consider doing this road in off hours—evenings or weekends.

Though the road is rough, the view of distant snowy mountains, the long narrow lakes (Ash, Turnbull and McLaughlin) that appear below to your left, and the river marked with white water make the trip worthwhile. **Just over 6.5 kilometres from the Ash River bridge, keep straight on, ignoring a road that heads left, up a hill, into active logging territory: watch for off-road trucks here.** Elsie Lake appears on the right soon after. This long, narrow body of water was once dammed to provide water for hydroelectric production; the grey stumps that poke up from the dry lake margins provide visible and ugly evidence of the change in the lake level.

Ash Main degenerates in this area, but should still be passable for an ordinary car, provided you take care, watch for potholes, and don't try to set speed records. No promises, though: the condition of disused roads can change from week to week. **Continue to the end of Elsie Lake, cross the Ash River once more, then keep a sharp eye out for an acute right on what looks like an overgrown track. Make a right here, to double back along Elsie Lake's north shore, on a road marked 124 on MacBlo's map. Set your trip odometer to zero, or make a note of your mileage here, since subsequent turns are measured from this point.**

You might want to walk the first few hundred metres of this road before you venture onto it with your car: this is the worst, though one of the prettiest stretches on this circle tour, with trees overarching and grass growing down the middle of the road. Bear scat decorates the verges and grouse flee, startled, into the underbrush. As you continue along the road parallel to the lake shore, notes and signs on styrofoam plates mark places where various groups camp.

Seven kilometres from the acute turn, the road crosses—or, at least, it is supposed to—a bridge where the timbers are rotting away. Walk the bridge to check for holes and make your own decision about whether it

Crossing a dilapidated bridge—very much an at-your-own-risk endeavour— north of Elsie Lake.

will support your car before you drive it. Proceed only with caution: there's no guarantee the timbers will survive another winter. If the bridge is out, you must retrace your route.

If you make it across the bridge, you've passed the worst of the tour. **Keep straight on across a second bridge—which should be in better condition—about 2.4 kilometres farther on. At 11.1 kilometres from the turn onto this road, keep left** (unless you want to make a stop on the shore of Elsie Lake). About 1.5 kilometres beyond, watch to your right to spot an old logging railway trestle now almost hidden in the undergrowth.

At 14.4 kilometres, keep right: the left fork takes you towards the Comox Valley. The dream of a Valley Link Highway is not a new one; residents of both valleys have been agitating for a road link since the 1880s, and the British Columbia Directory of 1893 reported a trunk road from Port Alberni to Beaver Creek "is being carried on to Comox." Every year, a cavalcade of vehicles makes the trip on logging roads to publicize the possible route.

At 17.5 kilometres, keep right down the hill; at 18.7 keep straight on (left links you to the Comox Road). Note the "Future Valley Link Highway" sign in the bushes. **Keep right at the next three possible lefts,** passing now through a pretty forest of Douglas-fir, salal, ferns, and Oregon grape. **Keep left at 25.1 kilometres, to cross a creek into a clearing 1.5 kilometres farther on. Keep right at 28.2 kilometres, continuing to an intersection with Beaver Creek Road .7 kilometres on.**

If you want a break from driving and would like to go for a hike along the grade of an old logging railway, turn left here and make an immediate right on Wolseley, to reach a small parking area and a sign that indicates the entrance to the 20-kilometre Log Train Trail, along the route of the old Alberni Pacific Lumber Company railways. To continue back towards Port Alberni, **turn right on Beaver Creek Road.** This paved road traces a path across farm fields with the mountains showing blue across the valley.

Beaver Creek Road slices through the farmlands of the Alberni basin, 40 kilometres long, 8 to 11 kilometres wide, a valley caught between the Beaumont Range to the east, the Vancouver Island mountains to north and west. The only low-lying area in this jumble of mountains, it attracted settlers as early as the 1880s, who cleared the land and established the farms you see today. Once Stamp's lumber mill closed, lumbering virtually

The McLean Mill

In 1925, R.B. McLean started up a small, family-operated logging business in the Beaver Creek Valley. For forty years, the McLeans ran a steam-driven sawmill at the camp where the family and a number of the workers lived.

In 1965, the era of steam long past, this last surviving steam-powered mill in B.C. closed, and houses, machinery, and mill settled into the undergrowth. But the mill was little disturbed over the next two decades, and, when the McLeans donated the mill and machinery to Port Alberni, it was still possible to begin restoration of this historic site.

Since then, the McLean Mill has been declared a national historic site, MacMillan Bloedel has donated 13 hectares of land around the mill, the buildings have been stabilized, and efforts are underway to restore some of the mill site.

Those efforts are by no means complete, and you won't find costumed actors or tour guides to show you what everything means. That's part of the mill site's charm: you can gawk at the steam-driven line shaft system through gaps in the mill wall, admire the heritage heavy industrial vehicles restored by members of the Western Vancouver Industrial Heritage Society, and imagine what it might have been like to sleep in the bunkhouse as the rain dripped down on the roof, eat in the cookhouse, or repair machinery on the green chain or in the planer mill.

ended in this region, and it was farmers who founded the waterside community of Alberni near the mouth of the Somass River. Decades later, lumbering and paper mills were re-established where they now stand, and the community around them named Port Alberni. After years of alternate co-operation and feuding, the two communities merged in 1967.

Just over 6 kilometres along Beaver Creek Road, on your right, is the entrance to Stamp Falls Provincial Park. A short trail from the parking lot leads to Stamp Falls and the fish ladders installed to help salmon ascend the river to spawn in fall. The stream is a perfect place to dangle your feet—or immerse yourself—on a hot summer's day.

Continue 7.3 kilometres along Beaver Creek Road and turn left on Smith Road. Smith leads 3 kilometres to the McLean Mill, a 1930s steam-driven lumber mill now being restored as a national historic site.

Return to Beaver Creek Road and continue towards Port Alberni. Six kilometres from Smith Road, Beaver Creek Road intersects Highway 4. Turn right for west-coast points, left for Port Alberni and the east coast.

 **ALBERNI INLET AND NAHMINT LAKE**

This tour circles south of Highway 4, from Port Alberni and back again, along Alberni Inlet, then high into the mountains near the city, through logging country, along lakes and back to the highway. It showcases great views of the inlet and the mountain lakes. It's about a three-hour drive, with the usual number of stops.

Gravel most of the way, it can be difficult in places for passenger cars. **Note that drivers may have to retrace their path at one point instead of completing the circle.** A good summer evening drive—in fact, weekends and evenings may be the only time you can tackle these roads, since logging traffic can be heavy.

Before You Go

Check with MacBlo's Sproat Lake Division (724-4433). They rarely officially close the road, and a call may bring you the news that, yes, the road is open. But when you drop in en route at the division headquarters, someone may well suggest that logging truck traffic is heavy and travel not advised. Take their advice seriously. The best map reference is MacMillan Bloedel's *Recreation and Logging Road Guide to the Forest Lands of West Central Vancouver Island: Tree Farm Licence 44*, available from MacMillan Bloedel offices or from the Port Alberni Forest Information Centre, on Alberni Quay in downtown Port Alberni. The B.C. Forest Ministry's *Port Alberni Forest District Recreation Map* is also useful, though not as accurate or detailed as MacBlo's map.

☸ ☸ ☸

This route begins at the foot of Johnston Road, where Highway 4 turns right to parallel the Somass River and angle west to Tofino. Turn right with Highway 4, and continue west. Three kilometres from the foot of Johnston Road, you'll cross the Somass River by way of a grey bridge. **Immediately after the bridge, turn left on Mission Road.**

About a kilometre along, a road leads left into the J.V. Clyne Bird Sanctuary, where trumpeter swans and other waterfowl find homes at the mouth of the Somass River. Visible across the estuary and above Port Alberni is Mount Arrowsmith, 1,817 metres high, dominating the Alberni Valley. Like so many other places in British Columbia, the mountain is named for someone who never ventured across the Atlantic, let alone across the continent. The work of English cartographers Aaron and John Arrowsmith was, however, well known to Captain G.H. Richards, who surveyed and named much on and around Vancouver Island in 1858.

Continue along Mission Road, and bear right. Ahead on your left is the Sproat Lake headquarters of MacMillan Bloedel, where you can pick up maps and information on this and other back-road routes during office hours.

Beyond the headquarters, keep right at a junction signposted to Macktush campsite and Nahmint Lake; follow the Nahmint signs from now on. About 6.5 kilometres from the start of Mission Road, keep left, then keep left again, following the Nahmint signs. At 7.9 kilometres, turn left, again following the Macktush and Nahmint Lake signs. These roads, wide and good gravel, run through areas recently harvested and reforested. One sign along the way suggests the first harvest in this area dates back to 1886, a reference to early commercial logging on Vancouver Island.

The road swings down towards Alberni Inlet, where tugs tow log booms, and fishing boats, both commercial and sports, wend their way back and forth between marinas and favoured fishing spots. Alberni Inlet for years has been considered one of the best salmon-fishing locations in the world, a reputation underlined by major fishing derbies every year but threatened by the ever-dwindling Pacific salmon stocks.

At about 23.1 kilometres along the road to Nahmint Lake, Macktush Main slices right, up the valley gouged by Macktush Creek. **It is another half a kilometre to Bill Motyka Recreation Area,** a MacBlo campground and boat launch named for a long-time company employee. Though the broad flat space doesn't seem particularly inviting, it's crowded on summer weekends with boaters and fishers.

Half a kilometre past the campground, keep left, and continue along the edge of Alberni Inlet, passing through some interesting rock formations along the way—formations of a sort that could indeed make an accordion of your car. Where Nahmint Bay curves inward from the inlet, the road veers right, through firs and cedars and across creeks that tumble down in fall and winter, dry to a trickle in summer and early fall. Deep valleys plummet down from the road, and sheer slopes rise above. Though the views are superb, the road is not, and few cars continue past the inlet shore. The road could be particularly difficult in wet, muddy weather.

Nahmint Main climbs away from the inlet shore now, giving spectacular views of Nahmint River and Lake with the mountains beyond. Even at midsummer, cataracts tumble down the mountainside towards

Alberni Inlet

Alberni Inlet cuts almost due north from Barkley Sound, a 40-kilometre slash from the coast two-thirds of the way across Vancouver Island. Port Alberni, at the head of the inlet, is closer to the island's east coast than to the west coast.

Like other similar inlets cut in from the island's west coast, Alberni was gouged by glaciers making their way towards the ocean, then retreating to leave deep valleys filled over time by ocean water. It is one of the longest inlets on the island.

For both the natives who were Vancouver Island's original settlers and later comers, the inlet promised much. Salmon spawned in and returned to the streams that fed into the inlet, providing a food supply for all who lived along their banks. The protected waters of the inlet provided sites for winter villages and temporary camps.

Early non-native arrivals thought the inlet could be their route to riches. Named Canal de Alberni (*canal* can mean either channel or canal) by early Spanish explorer Francisco Eliza after a fellow Spaniard who planted the first garden at Nootka, the inlet seemed to some to be the perfect route for great ships that could carry away the wealth of the forests. It took many a year for that prophecy to be fulfilled, as the remoteness of the west coast and the difficulties of navigation delayed the building of a major port until well into the twentieth century.

Though the first mill closed for lack of easily accessible lumber, twentieth-century machinery and road-building technology made it much simpler to exploit the forest along the inlet's shores and logging camps were built, on shore and on stilts, usually at the mouths of rivers.

The inlet also provided huge catches of herring and salmon, and, from 1903 on, a number of salmon canneries and herring salteries were built along the shore. Alberni Inlet today is still known for its sports fishing, as conservation measures and hatchery-spawned fish begin to rebuild the declining salmon population.

The narrow confines and deep trough of the inlet can also bring disaster. In 1964, an earthquake near Anchorage, Alaska, created a massive uplift in the seafloor and sent a tidal wave coursing along the north Pacific coast, causing death and destruction along the Alaska coast. But the wave's energy was far from spent. Four hours later, a series of waves powered up Alberni Inlet and overflowed Alberni streets, throwing a freighter onto shore and fish boats into city streets. Log booms, boats, floats, houses, and debris: all surged forward with the waves. Alberni was the hardest hit of all Canadian coastal towns.

---

the river and lake, and it's easy to see why potholes and washboard occur.

At 53 kilometres, a small, almost invisible signpost points out a steep difficult trail to the lake. At 54.3 kilometres, just past the end of the lake, keep left and cross the Nahmint River, then keep left again on Riverside

Road to reach a campsite and canoe launch on the river at the head of the lake.

Return to Nahmint Main. This road now heads up a steep, washboarded hill that can pose a challenge to front-wheel-drive passenger cars. It's a challenge we didn't conquer, but returning along Nahmint Lake and the inlet back to Port Alberni was no hardship: the views from the road are worth seeing twice.

If your vehicle makes the hill, continue on Nahmint Main past Gracie Lake, to a junction with Stirling Arm Main. A right takes you back to MacBlo's Sproat Lake headquarters; turn left onto South Taylor Main and you'll parallel long, narrow Sproat Lake, then Taylor River, back to Highway 4 west of Port Alberni. Turn right to return to the city, left to continue on to west-coast points.

CHAPTER 4

The Comox Valley

THE COMOX VALLEY IS THE FARTHEST NORTH OF THE WIDE LOW-lands on the island's east coast, a gentle space centred on the Comox River and its branches, its face to the sea, its back to the mountains that rise abruptly to the island's centre. From Parksville north to Royston, the coastal plain is a narrow strip that barely has room for the houses, the tiny towns, and the businesses that crowd along the highway beside the Strait of Georgia. Then, at Royston, the lowland area widens into a fertile valley, the third of the island's good agricultural areas.

Not surprisingly, the Comox Indians made their homes along this area of the coast, building villages at the mouth of and along the major rivers, and camping where they could harvest fish or shellfish in season. The first white settlers arrived here, as they did in the Cowichan Valley, in 1862, drawn by reports of good agricultural land. Over the years, much of the land in the valley has been logged and the fertile lowlands converted to farms.

The valley today is centred on the twin towns of Courtenay and Comox—Comox, the older town, looking towards the ocean from the peninsula north of Comox Harbour; Courtenay, somewhat younger, built around land routes.

As in the other lowland areas, the Comox Valley back roads are of two types. The paved roads that circle from Courtenay around the Comox Peninsula, along the rivers, and back to Courtenay, follow the old routes linking farm to farm, settlement to settlement. The gravel roads that edge along the mountains and crowd the lakeshore were born as logging and mining roads.

The first tour in this section follows the paved roads; the second, mostly on gravel, reaches the old coal-mining town of Cumberland, then cuts through logging land and up the mountains.

Resources

The *Comox Valley Regional Map*, sponsored by the Comox Valley Ground Search and Rescue Association, sold at the tourist information centre and local stores, covers this area well and in detail. The *Campbell River Forest District Recreation Map* is available from Ministry of Forests offices. The Comox Valley Chamber of Commerce office and Tourist Infocentre is open year-round on the east side of Highway 19, at the south end of Courtenay. Watch for tourist information signs.

TOUR 13 THE COMOX PENINSULA

This tour follows paved roads along Comox Harbour through the town of Comox, then along the Strait of Georgia around the peninsula. It skirts the Comox Armed Forces Base, cutting through farmland to parallel the water again. It then turns inland and crosses the island highway north of Courtenay, to return through more farmland to its starting point.

En route are nature sanctuaries, pioneer pub, heritage lodge with gardens, sandy spit, long shingle beaches, farm markets, gentle country roads, fine views of the Strait of Georgia and the Vancouver Island and mainland mountains. The tour is suitable for all vehicles and drivers, good for cyclists, an all-season route.

Before You Go

The best map is the *Comox Valley Regional Map* listed at the beginning of this chapter, available from infocentres and area stores. Food, drink, and other commodities are available at many places along the route. Beach-walking shoes are a good idea.

☻ ☻ ☻

This tour begins at the junction of 17th Street and Cliffe Avenue, Highway 19, where the highway turns east across the Puntledge River for Comox and points north. Turn east to cross the bridge, following signs for Comox. At the T at the end of the bridge, turn right, for Comox. You are now on Comox Road. This road originally ran atop a dyke built to contain the waters of the river; old-timers in the area still call it Dyke Road.

Trumpeter Swans in the Comox Valley

In the 1930s, the death knell was sounded for trumpeter swans. Hunted and killed in great numbers, their habitat destroyed, the swans were then so few that most biologists thought they were headed for certain extinction.

But the efforts of those who thought the world would be a better place if these huge white birds were still around have brought them back from the edge. And every year, as hundreds of trumpeters gather in the Comox Valley, people gather to watch them.

Comox Harbour is a wintering and staging area for waterfowl, gulls, alcids, and grebes. Up to 12,000 birds of 112 species gather on the 900 hectares of water and surrounding marsh and shores. None is more magnificent than the trumpeter, which has a wingspan of up to 2.3 metres.

In 1963, a Christmas bird count found four trumpeter swans in the Comox area. Twenty years later, there were more than 700, a number that continues to climb. Now, more than fifteen per cent of the world's trumpeter population gathers here each winter.

The swans, distinguishable from other swans by their all-black bill (in mature birds) and the fact that their necks kink at the base when they are resting, also feed on farm fields around the Comox Peninsula. Many area farmers have joined the bid to protect the swans, leaving stubble in the fields where the swans come to feed.

Best time to see the swans is between late November and mid-March. Comox holds a swan festival in mid-February. By April, the birds have left for their nesting grounds in coastal and south-central Alaska.

Trumpeter swans hold a meeting near Dove Creek Road, not far from Courtenay.

(Gary Green photo)

Just over a kilometre from the bridge, you'll see signs for a wildlife viewing centre. **Turn right and park beside the viewing platform.** Every year in October, trumpeter swans begin to gather in the Comox Valley. By midwinter, there are more swans here than anywhere else in the world.

Continue along the river estuary as it widens into Comox Harbour. While the flats at the river mouth have long attracted wintering wildfowl, the harbour itself has been more important to humans. The Pentlatch and Comox native people lived beside the harbour, and fished and collected shellfish from its waters. The word *comox* means plenty, or abundance; salmon, shellfish, and game birds were abundant in the harbour at various times of the year.

White settlers who arrived in the 1860s found what they considered the essentials for a good settlement: safe anchorage for their ships, protected behind the spit that reaches out at the head of the harbour, backed by land that looked most promising for agriculture. In 1862, a wave of settlers arrived to take up land along the harbour.

Now, the harbour shore is home to fishboats, fish markets, and to an Indian reserve on the traditional territory of the Comox people. The Big House, on your left as you drive through the reserve, is used for native and cross-cultural events.

Follow Comox Avenue through the downtown area of Comox. Stop if you're thirsty for a beer at the Lorne Hotel, on your left in the centre of town. The clapboard and gingerbread Lorne, graced by a fine wide verandah, dates back to 1878—though its record of service is not unbroken. When British Columbia briefly went dry after World War I, the Lorne closed until it could serve alcohol again.

A right turn at the four-way stop onto Port Augusta Street will take you down to the docks where you can sit on a bench and regard fishboats, pleasure boats, and Sunday sailors. A fishing/viewing pavilion parallels the boat basin; there are several restaurants and a pub near the docks.

Continue south along Comox Avenue. About .5 kilometres from the Lorne Hotel, you'll reach the junction of Comox and Pritchard Road. Continue straight on, then turn right at the marked entrance to the Filberg House parking lot.

Robert Joseph Filberg arrived in the Comox Valley in 1916 to become superintendent of the Comox Logging and Railway Company, a subsidiary of a larger logging company owned by his father-in-law. Filberg and wife Florence moved to this house they had built in about 1929, in arts and crafts style. True to his timbering background, Filberg had the house built of wood and more than a hundred varieties of trees were planted on the grounds. A petroglyph thought to have come from a nearby beach is embedded in the lodge's fireplace. In August, the grounds are the site of a giant arts and crafts fair; at any time of year, you may see wedding parties posing for their formal photographs in the gardens.

Return to the junction of Comox and Pritchard, and turn onto Pritchard. Two hundred metres along Pritchard, turn right at a four-way stop onto Balmoral. A further 600 metres along, continue straight onto Hawkins Road, following it out onto Goose Spit.

The spit is mentioned in almost every seaborne expedition to the Comox area, but is little known to tourists who arrive by land. Goose Spit spears out from the bottom of a hill, a narrow sandy hook that probably began to form at the end of the last ice age, growing over time as the sea deposited sediments probably picked up as nearby cliffs eroded. As waves breached the spit over time, they deposited more sand on the inner side, making the spit wider and almost enclosing the area of shallow water between the spit and the shore.

The Puntlatch and Comox native peoples found the spit a good place to camp while they gathered shellfish. The Royal Navy used the spit as a base in colonial times, and a naval base operated here until 1947. The end of the spit is still used for a naval cadet camp. Comox Valley residents flock to the spit on warm days, to lounge under umbrellas on the long sand beach, and look across the water at the shadowy mountains beyond. Even in cooler weather, the spit is popular for picnics or beach walks.

Return back up Hawkins Road to the stop sign, and turn right. Make an immediate right onto Lazo Road. This route is marked by blue and white scenic-route signs, stylized representations of water and

Sunshine, sea, and mountains at Goose Spit in Comox.

mountains. Continue along Lazo Road, following it through a 90-degree turn to the left, then curving to the right back down to the water's edge.

Though no visible point spears out from the coastline, this area is known as Point Holmes, named before the middle of the nineteenth century by one of the survey ships in the region. A long extent of shingle beach looks southeast along the Strait of Georgia; less crowded in the summer than sandier, more sheltered beaches to the north and south, it's a pleasant place to linger.

Curve left up the hill, then turn right onto Kye Bay Road. To your left now are views across the edge of CFB Comox, over camas meadows that bloom blue in the spring towards the mountains behind Courtenay. This road swings back down to the water at Kye Bay, long a favourite summer spot for families with its jumble of summer cottages and cabins, a simple resort or two, and a park for day visitors beside the sandy beach with its warm, sheltered waters.

Return back along Kye Bay Road, and turn right at the stop sign. Continue north on what has become Knight Road. On your right, high fences mark the airfields of CFB Comox. To your left, farm fields and woods stretch towards the mountains. In summer, you can stop for Mother's Potatoes or sweet corn, for lettuces and carrots, for any of the produce grown nearby and sold at farm stands beside this road. In winter, trumpeter swans dine off the farmer's remnants.

Four kilometres from the Kye Bay Road intersection, turn right at a stop sign onto Military Row, marked on most maps as Little River Road. Behind the chain-link fence, military airplanes old and new are lined up, no longer active but on display for passersby. Among the aircraft are an Argus CP 107, a CF-100 Canuck, a CP-121 Tracker, a CF-104 Starfighter, and a C-47 Dakota, some of them types flown by squadrons that have been stationed at CFB Comox, others of special interest to aircraft aficionados.

Beyond the field aircraft on your right is the Comox Air Force Museum, open weekends throughout the year, plus Wednesday through Friday in summer. CFB Comox opened in 1943 as a Royal Air Force aerodrome, and was a transport operational training unit until the end of World War II. Closed in 1946, it reopened in 1952, and has served as a Canadian air base ever since. The museum focuses on the patrol, search and rescue, fighter-interceptor, naval and other squadrons that have been based at CFB Comox.

Continue straight on at the stop sign by the base entrance (the airplane on your right at the entrance is a CF-101 Voodoo, a supersonic, all-weather interceptor) **onto Little River Road. Turn right onto Kilmorley Road, about 1.7 kilometres from the intersection,** to a pub that is a popular lunch stop for civilians and base residents. **Continue on Kilmorley, then turn left on Astra/Booth Road,** which leads past Kin Beach Park, on the waterfront with good views of the Strait of Georgia and Powell River across the strait. **Turn right at the stop sign, back onto Little River Road, then turn left on Wilkinson Road. Follow Wilkinson about another kilometre to a stop sign. A right turn takes you to the ferry dock for the ferry to Powell River. Turn left, on Ellenor Road, then make an acute right turn 1.4 kilometres along onto Anderton Road.**

Anderton cuts through farm and forest, with valley and mountain views on your left, then swings onto Waveland Road, to cross through orchards and more farms. **Continue on Waveland Road to Bates Road, and turn left.** Bates Road takes you to and through Seal Bay Nature Park. You can park here, and wander along some of the 24 kilometres of nature trails. Trails to the right of the road lead along a ravine and through forest to the beach. Trails to the left of the road take you through forest to a swamp where waterfowl paddle and feed in the shallows.

Continue north on Bates Road, passing Bates Beach and a number of resorts. **About 2.5 kilometres from Seal Bay park, swing left with the main road,** which now becomes Coleman, a nicely rural road bordered by apple trees, woods, and home-based businesses that range from a hairdresser to a honey farm, and **continue another 4.3 kilometres to Highway 19.** About halfway along this road, you can make a right turn onto Left Road, then a right onto Whitaker, to reach Kitty Coleman Beach, a popular base for fishing and camping. Retrace your route back to Coleman. When you reach the highway, you can turn left for the direct route back to Courtenay, or right for Campbell River or to continue the back-road route.

To finish the back-road circle tour: turn right on the highway, then make the next left, onto Merville Road. Merville was named for a French town where Canadian soldiers fought in World War I. A number of Canadian soldiers were resettled here after the war, battling poor soil, stumps left behind by logging, and stony ground, before they were finally defeated by a massive fire that raced across their land.

Turn left about 2 kilometres along onto Headquarters Road. This road once had pretensions: it led from Courtenay to Headquarters, a company town near the meeting of the Tsolum River and Wolf Creek that was to be the main base of the Comox Logging and Railway Company. In 1910 and 1911, the company built service shops for their locomotives and cars, and housing for their employees and families beside the Tsolum River. Headquarters had it all—tennis court, hotel, Chinese laundry, Japanese store, school. But the mill built at Headquarters never started up; logs were shipped instead to mills on the Fraser River, and when railways gave way to trucks, Headquarters was closed down in 1958. The houses were sold for a dollar each, provided they were moved within a month. Virtually no sign remains today of the town.

Headquarters Road leads arrow-straight some 8 kilometres through farm fields, with a view of the mountains to the west, back towards the centre of Courtenay. As it nears the Tsolum River, it begins to twist and turn a little. Just past the intersection with Dove Creek Road, on the right, are the Comox Valley Exhibition Grounds, home on a September weekend to the Comox Valley Fall Fair. Saturday mornings May through October, valley farmers sell valley vegetables, berries, herbs and baked goods in a field beside the fairgrounds.

Follow Headquarters Road to the traffic lights where it meets the Island Highway. Turn right to reach Courtenay downtown, left to head towards Campbell River, straight on to return to the tour starting point at the end of the bridge across the Comox River.

 ## CUMBERLAND TO COURTENAY

This tour traces early routes from the water at Royston to the old mining town of Cumberland, then cuts north through the rough country at the foot of the mountains, behind Courtenay, on mostly gravel logging roads. It includes several options: you can spend a full day or more exploring, bypassing Courtenay completely, or you can choose one of several shorter routes that loop from the water to the mountains and back to Courtenay. Depending on the options you choose, the tour can take from a few hours to a full day.

This tour is suitable for most cars and drivers who don't mind gravel. Some parts are suitable for cyclists. The routes around Courtenay are accessible in winter; the route south along Comox Lake may or may not be—check locally.

En route are local mining history, small-town ambling, river and lakeside picnicking, superb views out over the valley and the strait, possibilities for mountain meadow hiking.

Before You Go

If you plan to spend much time in this area, get the combined Courtenay/ Comox city and regional map—it includes logging and hiking trails and is sponsored by the local Chamber of Commerce and the Comox Valley Ground Search and Rescue Association. It's for sale at the Chamber of Commerce office and local stores. Off-season, many amenities are closed, so a supply of food and drink is a good idea. Take along the usual logging road emergency equipment if you plan to follow the gravel road along Comox Lake or north to Campbell River.

⊛ ⊛ ⊛

The tour begins on Highway 19 south of Courtenay, in the small village of Royston. **Turn west, away from the water, onto Royston Road, signposted for Cumberland.**

This pleasant paved road runs through rural country: small farm fields with horses nodding over the fences, cabins half-hidden in the woods, larger houses where suburbia is spreading south from Courtenay. Six kilometres from Royston, it reaches Cumberland.

A small and fairly sleepy town now, Cumberland has a tumultuous past. A rich seam of coal was discovered near here in 1864. Coal and railway magnate Robert Dunsmuir bought out the claims in 1883, but it was not until 1888 that mining actually began. A railway was built to

Restored mine-town buildings on Dunsmuir Avenue, in Cumberland.

link the mines with wharves at Union Bay, and the new town took the name of Union. Five years later, forest was cleared for the neighbouring town which became Cumberland.

The mining town followed the usual pattern of mining boom towns in B.C.: quick growth as miners and their families moved in and businesses were established. In 1897, Cumberland was incorporated as a city— albeit the smallest city in North America at the time. The town grew and coal production continued through the 1920s, but then fell off. When the last mine closed in 1966, it was simply the acknowledgement of what had been obvious for almost forty years: Cumberland's mining times were over. Today, it has a population of some 2,000.

Royston Road becomes Dunsmuir Avenue, the town's main street, which provides a pleasant stroll past or into small stores and cafes. The museum is at the corner of Dunsmuir and First Street, beside a reconstructed row of colourful, false-fronted, turn-of-the century buildings. Pick up a walking tour map at the Chamber of Commerce office on Dunsmuir or at the museum, and take a look at the old Japanese, Chinese, and black townsites, the miners' cemeteries, and other evidence of the mining past.

If you want to take a break on the shore of Comox Lake, continue along Dunsmuir Avenue to Sutton Street, then turn left down the hill and follow the signs to the lake, past the old Japanese townsite, one-time Chinatown, and several of the old mine locations.

Backtrack along Dunsmuir Avenue and turn left on Fourth Street, heading up the hill behind the town. Fourth becomes Cumberland Road; just after the road curves to the right, turn left onto Bevan Road. Follow Bevan Road to a stop sign at a gravel road.

From this point, you can drive to the north shore of Comox Lake, where you can picnic beside the Puntledge River, then return towards Courtenay. This logging road along the lake continues, should you want to go that far, to the Port Alberni area.

Optional: to make this trip or some part of it, you should carry with you the logging road maps mentioned at the beginning of this chapter, plus those listed in the Port Alberni tours. Turn left at the stop sign and follow gravel Comox Lake Main to the head of Comox Lake. Continue straight on across the Puntledge River/Comox Lake dam and turn right (signposted) to the BC Hydro Comox Lake Dam picnic site. Or, continue straight, along the north shore of Comox Lake.

Over the past year or two, Comox Lake Main beyond the Puntledge

The Cumberland Miners

From photograph after photograph in the Cumberland museum, the faces stare back: whites, Chinese, Japanese, blacks, miners who worked at the Cumberland mines. And sometimes the faces express what many of these men must have felt much of the time: anger and frustration at the treatment meted out to them by the colliery bosses and owner Robert Dunsmuir.

The early decades of the twentieth century saw angry confrontations across North America between the bosses, who were convinced that unfettered capitalism was the rightful way of a rapacious society, and the workers, who were just beginning to band together in unions that battled for greater safety, higher wages, and better working conditions. A clash between Dunsmuir, formed in the bullheaded capitalist mould, and his workers was inevitable.

Safety was a primary issue: close to 300 miners were killed in Cumberland mine explosions and cave-ins between the 1880s and the 1920s. Wages were another. The use of Chinese and Japanese miners was another—connected to the question of wages, since Dunsmuir paid his non-white workers less than half what he paid white workers.

In 1912, Cumberland miners went on strike, primarily for safer working conditions; Nanaimo miners soon followed. The government sided with the mine owners, sending soldiers to end the strike. Chinese and Japanese miners were forced back to work with threats of deportation, and the mines reopened.

But the strife was far from over. In 1918, the police shot socialist union leader Albert "Ginger" Goodwin, who was hiding out in the hills behind Cumberland.

On Goodwin's funeral day, Cumberland miners formed a parade more than a kilometre and a half long, and marched through town streets. Unions across B.C. called for a one-day "holiday" to protest the shooting. The strike led to violence in Vancouver and elsewhere. The open wounds between labour, company management and owners, and the government would not heal easily.

River has often been closed for active logging (sometimes helicopter logging) or for bridge replacement and repair. It can also be rough in sections. Back roads and trails off Comox Lake Main lead to the Comox Glacier area; trails lead across to Buttle Lake and into Strathcona Provincial Park.

If Comox Lake Main is open, continue along the lakeshore; you'll cross various creeks and rivers, including, about three-quarters of the way along the lake, the Cruikshank River, which has now been spanned by a new bridge. About 4 kilometres past this bridge, beyond the end of the lake and immediately after a bridge across a smaller creek, turn left, cross a small bridge, then keep right after a second small bridge across Toma Creek, to join up with Toad Lake Road to Port Alberni (see Tour 11).

Return to the junction of Bevan Road and Comox Lake Main. Continue on the extension of Bevan Road, crossing Comox Lake Main and heading northwest. This road curves past the North Comox Lake hostel, near the site of the short-lived town of Bevan. In 1911–12, some 150 houses were home to miners who worked a nearby mine. When production declined, the houses were sawn in half, transported to Cumberland by rail, and put back together again.

The road now becomes Lake Trail Road, a paved public road. It recrosses Comox Lake Main; **continue on Lake Trail, then take the first left past Marsden Road, back onto Comox Lake Main, which will become Duncan Bay Main.** From this point on, the route is a recognized cycling route: though the occasional gravel portion may jar you, most of the route is suitable for cyclists. Watch for logging trucks on this road; about a kilometre along, beware of serious speed bumps—not flagged—that warn that you are entering a logging company yard. Continue through the yard, bearing right, into the Oyster River Managed Forest, then cross the Puntledge River about 1.6 kilometres from the logging yard. The river here is worth a stop, especially at low water, when you can walk along the large flat stones that border the water.

About 1.8 kilometres past the bridge, you once more have options. You can cut short the back-roading and head for Courtenay; this is the recognized cycling route. Or, you can continue on to the roads that climb to Forbidden Plateau and Mount Washington.

To return to Courtenay: turn right onto Piercey Road. Piercey emerges from the forest into wide farm fields populated with horses and dairy cows. **Continue on Piercey to a T-junction at Dove Creek Road; turn right and cross the Tsolum River. Turn right at the T, and follow Headquarters Road back to the island highway and Courtenay.**

To continue along the back roads west of town: turn left at the Piercey Road intersection, for Forbidden Plateau.

The gravel road curls up the mountain for about 15 kilometres, with fine views of Courtenay, the Strait of Georgia, and the mainland beyond. It ends at the parking lot for Forbidden's ski lodge and lifts. In winter, the lot is jammed with skiers' vehicles, and visitors skid back and forth between day lodge, lifts, and the RV campground. Off-season—from late

April till the snow falls—the area is less crowded. Between late June and early September, the chairlift is open for hikers who want to ride in comfort to a point 1,000 metres above the water below, and hike either further up the mountain or back down to the lodge. Trails from the top of the chair vary from a very easy 15-minute stroll to more difficult, overnight and longer trails that connect to the Strathcona Provincial Park network of trails and hiking routes.

Many stories are told about the past of Forbidden Plateau, in a time when the Comox area native peoples were the only human inhabitants of the valley. The area was "forbidden" because it harboured evil and mystery: one story suggests that a group of women and children sent into the plateau to escape from enemies was never seen again. Others suggest a tribe of vengeful giants lived on the plateau.

Whatever its past, it now attracts many who treasure the alpine flower meadows that bloom in August, the canyons, the alpine lakes, and the mountains that surround the plateau.

Return back down the mountain, and turn left back onto Duncan Bay Main, signposted to Mount Washington. The road crosses Browns River almost immediately, then continues north through logged and re-forested areas. Just after you cross a second bridge, over Dove Creek, you reach a stop sign at the road to Mount Washington.

Turn left to reach Mount Washington. The road climbs through switchbacks that offer fine views over the Strait of Georgia to the ski development high above the valley. Like Forbidden Plateau, Mount Washington is busiest in winter, when thousands of skiers make day trips or stay overnight in the many condominiums that line the mountainside, eager to ride the five lifts to more than 20 ski runs, try the cross-country ski circuit, learn to ski, or practise après-ski in the lodge.

Off-season, visitors can camp, mountain bike, enjoy the views, hike the trails or—July to early September—ride the chair lifts to more views and more trails.

Return back to the Duncan Bay Main intersection and more options to complete your back-road trip at Courtenay, on the Island Highway north of Courtenay, or at Campbell River via a logging road.

• **To return to Courtenay: continue straight on from Mount Washington towards the water. Just over a kilometre from the intersection, turn right on Dove Creek Road.** This paved road leaves the forest behind for hayfields, riding rings, cornfields, and dairy pastures.

At Dove Creek Hall, just under 8 kilometres from its start, Dove Creek Road takes an abrupt left. Turn left here.

A kilometre or so along, keep an eye out on your right for McGinnis Berry Farms. The Comox Valley is justly famed for its farm produce, but even among the good foods of the valley, McGinnis day-neutral strawberries are something special. While most strawberries fruit when the days are longest, this type has been bred to fruit throughout the summer and into fall. These plants produce sweet red berries from June through October.

About 2.5 kilometres along, keep left with Dove Creek Road, across Dove Creek; in summer, you may want to join the locals lazing the day away with their feet in the river below the bridge. **At the stop sign, turn right onto Headquarters Road.**

On the right as you head into town are the Comox Valley fairgrounds, home each summer Saturday morning to a farmers' market where you can buy local produce that ranges from berries to corn to fancy lettuces to honey to prepared sauces and snacks. If you're lucky, you'll be here in late September, for the Comox Valley Fall Fair, one of the best on the

A display at the Comox Valley Fall Fair, at the fairgrounds on Headquarters Road.

island, when 4-H club members groom their charges, competitors vie for prizes for best everything from zucchini to pie to honey, and exhibitors proudly display a wide range of steam-driven machinery.

Continue on Headquarters Road; 1.6 kilometres past the fair-grounds, at a traffic light, is the Island Highway. A left turn takes you north towards Campbell River, a right turn into the heart of Courtenay's downtown, and straight on leads to points south.

• **To return to the Island Highway north of Courtenay from the intersection of Duncan Bay Main and the Mount Washington Road: continue straight on from Mount Washington, crossing Duncan Bay Main. Keep right on Farnham Road (gravel) 6.8 kilometres from the intersection, then continue straight on a further 2.8 kilometres to Howard Road. Turn left.** Howard Road cuts through forest and farm-land to return you to the Island Highway between Merville and Black Creek.

• **To reach Campbell River via the back road: continue north on Duncan Bay Main from the Mount Washington Road intersection.** In many ways, this logging road is a less interesting route north than is the paved Island Highway. It is for the most part wide and reasonably flat, somewhat dull, through second-growth forest with few breaks. Its virtue is that it is rarely crowded. It may, however, be open only after 6 p.m. on weekdays and on weekends. It is signposted as such from the Courtenay end, but not signposted from the Campbell River end.

About 7 kilometres along the route, Wolf Lake appears below the road on the right. Various rough roads lead down to the lake; take the one at about 8 kilometres to see the lake, where the remains of an old logging railway trestle still poke above the water.

At about 11 kilometres from the Mount Washington junction, keep right as Rossiter Main bears left. You'll cross a bridge across McKay Creek and notice signs along the way that indicate the age of the second-growth timber around you. Though it doesn't have a lot to offer passenger-car drivers, four-wheeler aficionados like the area: you'll see ATVs taking off into the bush, and trucks passing by with dirt bikes roped into the pickup beds.

About 24.7 kilometres from the Mount Washington junction, the road crosses a solid plank bridge over the Oyster River, a pleasant place for a stop to look at the rapids or sit by the rushing water. The pull-off here is a favourite marshalling place for ATVers, who arrive complete with fishing and camping gear.

Just past the bridge, keep left up the hill, continue straight on past the camp 1.4 kilometres farther on, and cross a second bridge. Turn left to stay on Duncan Bay Main and continue along this wide gravel road through forest. **At 32.4 kilometres, keep right (Gilson Main is to your left), continue under the power lines and past the back of the Campbell River airport, to emerge along the western edge of Campbell River.**

The road continues through scrub brush and logged areas that permit a view of the distant mountains. At 44.8 kilometres, you'll see a large TimberWest sign. **Turn right onto Willis Road, then left onto Peterson, to reach the Island Highway about 49 kilometres from the Mount Washington Road junction. A right turn on the highway takes you into Campbell River, a left to points north.**

CHAPTER 5

The North Island

NOT SO VERY LONG AGO, EVERY ROAD ON THE NORTHERN HALF of Vancouver Island could have been considered a back road. If you wanted to travel beyond Kelsey Bay, 65 kilometres north of Campbell River, you could fly, boat, or follow a rugged logging road out of Gold River on the west coast along the Gold and Nimpkish river valleys back across to Woss Camp and the east coast. Except for the short stretch of paved road connecting Port McNeill to Port Hardy, and the streets of the two towns, every road was gravel.

In 1978, the long-promised paved highway from Campbell River north to Port Hardy was opened, and thousands of people now drive the blacktop every year. But most of them are heading for the ferry to Prince Rupert, which now leaves from Port Hardy, and few stop to explore north island back roads.

That's either a shame or a blessing, depending on how you look at it. The many kilometres of dusty gravel roads that penetrate to old mining towns, logging camps both abandoned and thriving, west-coast fishing villages, and lonely stretches of ocean inlet are rarely busy and always worthwhile.

Geography and history dictate the routes of these roads. The north island has none of those friendly valleys that are the centres of south island population, and the coastal plain barely exists. Instead, this region is a geological jumble of rocky mountain chains, cleft river valleys, wild and lonely coastline, and evergreen forest, both logged and virgin. Little wonder that the Kwakwaka'wakw people who were the first occupants of this land relied heavily on the sea for their transportation routes, travelling by land only on such comparatively easy trade paths as that along the Nimpkish River. And little wonder, too, that early settlers tried to establish themselves on the coast, thinking even such isolated outposts as Cape Scott would prove more rewarding than anywhere in the interior.

Even today, almost all the north island's settlements are on the seacoast, the only exceptions being logging or mining camps that will probably disappear once their reason for existing is gone. The back roads of the north island cross from the east coast to the heads of the deep inlets that slash inland from the west coast, or follow logging routes across the interior. All are gravel roads. Among their attractions are superb views over these ocean inlets, glimpses of an age-old forest that once clothed all this land, limestone formations, tumbling rivers, and deep narrow lakes.

Resources

If you want to backroad in this country, you need maps. If you are on the North Island, you can find logging-company maps at logging-company offices; at the Forest Industry Information Centre in the centre of Campbell River (where the museum used to be, near Tyee Plaza); at the forest centre south of Port McNeill, almost opposite the Zeballos turn-off; or at tourist infocentres. However, if you are a dedicated backroader, you may find, as we did, that you are never near a town during office hours. Try phoning or writing to get copies of the company maps ahead of time.

Two non-company maps: *Northern Vancouver Island Recreation and Relief Map*, produced by G.M. Johnson and Associates Limited, 1994; sold in bookstores on the lower island. *Port McNeill Forest District Recreation Map*, available from Ministry of Forests offices throughout the province; good for general planning, but not great on specifics.

Company maps: *Recreation and Logging Road Guide to the Forest Lands of West Vancouver Island*, a Pacific Forest Products guide to the Gold River/ Zeballos area. (Pacific Forest Products, P.O. Box 220, Gold River, B.C. V0P 1G0; Tel. 604/283-2221; FAX 604/283-7222.) *Western Forest Products Visitors' Guide to Northern Vancouver Island*, excellent for anything north or west of Port McNeill. Available from infocentres and WFP offices, or call WFP at 604/956-4446. *Recreation and Logging Road Guide to Forestlands of Northern Vancouver Island: Port McNeill/Port Hardy* and *Campbell River/ Sayward*, both from MacMillan Bloedel and available from MacBlo offices or from the forest information centre in Campbell River. *Welcome to the Nimpkish Valley*, and *Englewood Logging Division, TFL 37*, both from Canadian Forest products at Woss, B.C. V0N 3P0; Tel. 604/281-2300; FAX 604/281-2485.

 ## NORTH OF CAMPBELL RIVER

Though Campbell River is just halfway up Vancouver Island, geographically it is part of the north island. The coastal plain here has slimmed to almost nothing, the mountains crowd in closer to the shore, and rushing rivers and small lakes are the dominant features of the landscape. The Sayward Forest, an area of forest and small lakes just north of Campbell River, has attracted lovers of the outdoors for many decades. Over the past few years, new trails, canoe routes, and interpretive signs have enhanced the area, and made it even more popular.

Gravel roads, most of them fair to good, make this tour suitable for most vehicles and drivers; bicyclists will probably prefer to drive in, then tackle a challenging mountain-bike circuit. Dusty in dry weather, can be muddy in wet; check to see if any of the roads have been ploughed in snowy times.

Along the way are lakeshore campsites, distant mountain views, elk habitat, a canoeing circuit, picnic areas, and historical and natural history interpretation.

Before You Go

The Ministry of Forests publishes an excellent series of maps and pamphlets on the area covered by this tour. The basic map is the *Campbell River Forest District* map. Also available are pamphlets, with maps, on the Sayward Forest Canoe Route; the Snowden Demonstration Forest recreation and interpretive trails; and Elk Habitat Management. These publications can be obtained from the ministry office at 370 South Dogwood Street, Campbell River, V9W 6Y7, Tel. 604/286-9300.

⋀ ⋀ ⋀

Begin at the junction of Highways 19 and 28 at the north end of Campbell River. Proceed west on Highway 28, towards Gold River. Several roads to the right lead to sections of Elk Falls Provincial Park, with trails and pleasant picnic areas. **At 4.5 kilometres from the highway 19/28 junction, bear right on the road signposted to Elk Falls Provincial Park and Loveland Bay. Cross the John Hart Dam. Where**

the road bears left to continue along John Hart Lake, keep right into Elk Falls park.

This picnic and day-use area is well worth visiting. The road curves down through giant Douglas-fir and hemlock to a parking lot. Trails lead from the lot to a series of waterfalls that wax and wane with the escapement of water from the dam. Elk Falls drops 25 metres; Moose Falls descends over a series of drops, the highest 10 metres.

Return to the main road and continue along John Hart Lake. Note the signs here and in the park that warn visitors of sudden and unexpected rises and drops in water level as water is retained then released at the dam. A siren indicates rising water levels.

No one thinks twice today about British Columbia's dependence on hydroelectric power from dams and powerhouses on river systems all across the province. But in the late 1920s, when talk was first heard about harnessing the Campbell River to produce power for industry, the mighty projects on the Peace and the Columbia were yet to come.

In fact, the first dams on the Campbell River were not built for another ten years. The John Hart Dam was completed in 1939, with added power coming on stream in 1949 and 1953. In the mid-fifties, conservationists protested at a proposed dam that would dramatically change the contours of the Campbell River system upstream from Campbell Lake. They won the battle but lost the war: the location of the dam was changed, so that not as much land as under the original proposal was flooded, but the bottom of the Elk Valley disappeared under the flood waters and the level of Buttle Lake was raised by 9 metres.

Some 6.5 kilometres from the highway, keep left on a gravel road following signs for Loveland Bay; the paved road continues straight ahead. You are now on Brewster Lake Road.

This good gravel road—with occasional washboarding—passes through Douglas-fir, fireweed, and alder. Stay on the main road (keep right at 12.6 kilometres, left at 13.6, right at 14.4) and on past a little lake that pops up on your left. If you are here in summer or fall, you'll undoubtedly see surveyor's bright ribbon or impromptu directional signs, printed on paper plates and tacked to trees. Each indicates a favourite camping spot or meeting place for a group, usually from Campbell River, who arrive in separate vehicles to spend a weekend or a few days fishing, hiking, and if the pictures on the signs mean anything, drinking case after case of beer.

At 17.2 kilometres, a spur road leads left to Loveland Bay Pro-

The Great Fire

Was a still-burning cigarette thrown into dry logging debris? Did sparks fall from a logging donkey engine or a steam locomotive on a logging railway? The question can't be answered. In scant minutes on July 5, 1938, flames ran through a small area around a logging camp near Campbell River.

Firefighters soon seemed to have the blaze under control. But the dry northwest wind that had been blowing for several days caught the fire and carried it on, away from the firefighters. Now a pall of smoke rose over an ever-growing area as the fire raced out from that first spark.

For a month, the flames spread, sweeping south almost to Comox Lake, consuming heaps of slash and piles of felled timber with indifference, jumping a gap of more than 2 kilometres across Campbell Lake. The fire became the second-largest ever in North America. More than 700 men battled the flames, felling dry snags in the fire's path, putting out spot fires, building fire guards, wielding hoses, and working pumps.

Unemployed men were conscripted from Vancouver to fight the fire. By mid-July many had had enough and sabotaged hoses and pumps. Their tactics worked, and they were sent back to Vancouver. In the Comox Valley, residents in the path of the fire hung their valuables on ropes they lowered into their wells, and fled to nearby beaches. Smoke obscured the sun and ash fell all along the coast.

By August 1, the fire had finally been contained, then extinguished after burning across more than 32,000 hectares. Some areas in the fire's path somehow escaped. As 1,500 firefighters tried to hold back the flames, the wind shifted, and the blaze raced away in another direction.

Though the fire caused enormous damage, it brought some good. Government and industry began to realize that current methods of leaving slash after logging, and slash-burning, were irresponsible. The government turned its attention to reforestation: in those days, loggers and government alike had blithely assumed the forest would regenerate by itself. That same year of 1938, the provincial government decided to establish a forest nursery near Campbell River. The next year, workers began replanting in the area.

---

vincial Park, a pretty, supervised (in season) camp and picnic site on the shore of Loveland Bay, on Campbell Lake. Stop for a picnic, or **continue on half a kilometre to a junction.**

Two routes are possible here. A shorter inner circle crosses Snowden Demonstration Forest, where you will find interpretive trails with signs that provide information on logging history, the area forest, and elk habitat. Route directions for this circle follow. A longer outer circle doesn't have the interpretive trails, but passes more campsites and lakes, and has the better views.

• **To follow the inner circle through the Snowden Demonstration Forest: turn right half a kilometre past Loveland Bay onto a partly overgrown road marked by a Snowden sign.** The Snowden Forest, like other demonstration forests on Vancouver Island, is intended as an outdoor demonstration of the human and natural history of the forest, coupled with information on present multiple uses—logging, recreational, wildlife—of the forest. This means you may meet a logging truck or see newly planted clear-cuts, but you'll also see trails with interpretive signs. In this particular demonstration forest, the Ministry of Forests is changing its focus from education to recreation, a trend evident in the maps of the canoe circuit and mountain biking trails here.

The main self-guided tour in the Snowden Forest goes by the name of "Trees, Trails and Trestles." Some signs indicating tour stops may be missing, and the boxes holding single-page trail guides may be empty, so it helps if you have already obtained the relevant pamphlets from the forest service office in Campbell River.

Drive northeast on Snowden Road. The first four stops on the tour are all on the right side of the road. This road follows the old mainline of a logging railway built in 1929. The old-growth timber all logged off by the early 1950s, the line was abandoned and the tracks removed. In 1985, the mainline route was upgraded.

The Greenstone herd of about a hundred Roosevelt elk frequent the area. An elk habitat management tour points out important sites in habitat management, explaining the food and cover requirements of the elk herd. Stop 3 is at the beginning of one of three educational trails the Forest Service has developed for school students. The 325-metre forest trail has signs that help identify trees, plants of the forest floor, wildlife, and other parts of the old-growth forest: this small area has not been logged.

Just north of the old forest trail is an ecosystem trail, 800 metres along a bog, past rocky areas, and through second-growth forest. The trail guide reveals how natural and unnatural events have affected the ecology of the forest. The third trail, about 1.5 kilometres northeast of the ecosystem trail, to the right of Snowden Road, is a silviculture trail, 1,130 metres long, intended to show how silviculturists make decisions on replanting logged areas and tending the trees as they grow towards maturity.

Almost opposite the beginning of the ecosystem trail is a sign that tells the story of Mennonite settlers, given conscientious objector status in World War II, who reforested this area between 1942 and 1944. Also along Snowden Road (most other stops are to the left of the road) are areas where old tall stumps still show the notches that held the springboards used in 1930s logging; clear-cuts; a rock bluff that demonstrates the age-old effect of the advance and retreat of glaciers; and other notes on logging and reforestation.

After Stop 10, a side road to the right just past a creek crossing leads to several parking lots on the route of mountain bike trails that crisscross an area of the forest. Keep an eye out for Stop 12, on the left. This is Suicide Bridge, a long curved trestle that challenged locomotive engineers and brakemen as they made the downhill run to the booming grounds at Menzies Bay, hauling up to thirty railcars loaded with timber. More precisely, this is half of Suicide Bridge: the other half collapsed in the winter of 1994.

Nine kilometres from the beginning of the demonstration forest, Snowden Road meets the Iron River Mainline.

Option 1: Turn right here to return via a wide but busy gravel road to Highway 28. This route takes you past the Campbell River Nursery; 16 million Douglas-fir seedlings leave this nursery yearly to be planted throughout the province. **Just over 3 kilometres past the nursery, keep right on a paved road, and cross the Campbell River, reaching the junction with Highway 28 a kilometre from the beginning of the paved road. Turn left for Campbell River, right for Strathcona Provincial Park and Gold River.**

Option 2: From the Snowden Road/Iron River Mainline junction: turn left, then left again at a T-junction on Menzies Mainline, then make an immediate right on Highway 19 to return to Campbell River.

• To make the outer circle drive from the four-way junction of the Brewster Lake Road, Snowden Road, Camp 5 Road, and Lower Campbell Lake Road, turn left onto Lower Campbell Lake Road. The road narrows a little now, with old rail trestles sometimes visible. Mountain peaks, glaciers, and Lower Campbell Lake appear and disappear through the trees that crowd in on the road. Keep a watch out for canoeists hustling their craft across the road: a portage route on the 47-kilometre Sayward Forest canoe route crosses from Campbell Lake to Gosling Lake. This circuit, recommended in spring and fall, takes three to four days to complete, though most paddlers choose to do only a portion of the route.

The Forest Service maintains a number of campsites along this route, most of them good places to stop for an hour or longer. The Forest Service map for the Campbell River district helps here. Although all the campsites were probably marked at one time or another, many of the signposts have disappeared, whether through natural causes or through someone's desire to keep a favourite site a secret from casual droppers-by.

One such site is located between Fry and Gray lakes, a left turn about 30.7 kilometres from the highway. **Continue straight on, onto Gray Lake Road.** A further 1.2 kilometres along Gray Lake, a campsite is located off to the left; another .8 kilometres along, you can bear left on a bridge across the narrow tail of Brewster Lake to another camp/picnic site.

Keep right on the main road, now named Menzies Mainline, away from Brewster Lake and past marshy land on your left. The road snakes through forest, past favourite meeting places and unofficial campsites on small lakes tucked away from traffic. A left 5.7 kilometres from the tail of Brewster Lake leads to campsites on Brewster Lake; note that this access road may be moved another 600 metres farther along the road.

Continue along Menzies Mainline, then turn left at the signposted road to Morton Lake Provincial Park. This well-loved campsite is packed on holiday weekends and on many summer weekdays, and getting a campsite is difficult. Picnicking is another matter. The 6.5-kilometre road to the park leads through forest. Use caution here: at least one RV driver hastening to the campground lost his transmission fluid when he went too quickly over a rocky bump. The attraction at the end of the road is two lakes. Mohun is the much larger, ideal for canoeing; Morton, the smaller, is good for children's activities. Various trails lead along the lakeshores and into the forest.

Return to Menzies Mainline and continue east. The road is now wide and flat, better than almost any other gravel back road you'll discover on the north island, but heavily used by industrial traffic during the week: watch for extra-wide, off-highway logging trucks. Ten kilometres past the Morton Lake turn-off, you'll reach Highway 19. **Turn right for a scenic drive back to Campbell River, left for north island points.**

 **TO ZEBALLOS AND FAIR HARBOUR**

Like most others on the north island, this tour follows gravel roads along river valleys through forest, curving past the peaks of the Vancouver Island mountain chain. It reaches the heads of three fjord-like inlets that cut deep into the coastline, one of which is the jumping-off point for kayakers and other waterborne explorers of Kyuquot Sound; explores a 1930s gold-mining town reborn as a logging and fishing town; and shows you picturesquely eroded limestone formations.

This is definitely a full day's trip, which could easily extend into a second day if you decide to explore other area logging roads. Services are available only at Zeballos, so take food, drink, and emergency supplies. If you have car problems, it will be a long hike out to find help.

Suitable for most cars and drivers who are willing to tackle gravel roads that may be potholed and bumpy. Not suitable for large RVs. Not suitable for bicyclists, unless dust is your preferred meal—though a group of bicycling seniors from the Parksville area did persuade the crew of the ship *Uchuck* to land them at Zeballos. Half of the group hitched a ride on a van, prearranged, while the others rode the dusty road back to the Island Highway.

Best in spring and fall; like most gravel roads, these ones are dusty in good weather, muddy in bad. Along the way are limestone caves and arches, stunning silhouettes of mountain and forest, deep green inlet waters, a sleepy small town with ca. 1935 pub, and lovely views of coastline. Enquire locally for current conditions: bridges may be under repair, and industrial traffic will probably be using the road. The main road to Zeballos is a public road, always open. Other roads are usually open. Not recommended in winter.

Before You Go

Two logging company maps are helpful here. Canfor's Nimpkish Valley map covers the area from the highway through to Atluck Lake, while Pacific Forest Products' *Recreation and Logging Road Guide to the Forest Lands of West Vancouver Island* takes you to Zeballos and Fair Harbour. It may be possible to cross from the Zeballos road to reach Port Alice via the back door. If you want to try this trip—we were unable to do so since the main bridge was out—you also need MacMillan Bloedel's logging road guide to the Port Hardy/Port McNeill area, and Western Forest Products Northern Vancouver Island guide.

☿ ☿ ☿

The tour begins on Highway 19, 151 kilometres north of Campbell River, 43 south of the Port McNeill turn-off. **Turn west on the road signposted for Zeballos: it cuts back parallel to the highway for a few hundred metres, and is easily identified by the *Welcome to Zeballos* billboard near the highway. Continue on this road.**

About 2 kilometres along, you'll cross the Nimpkish River on a high bridge. **Keep right across the bridge, on the road signposted for Zeballos. Some 3.3 kilometres from the highway turn-off, about a kilometre after the river bridge, turn right on a road which should be signposted to Anutz Lake and Little Hustan Caves Regional Park. Note that from now on, signs direct you to *Huson* Park. Keep left a further 2.5 kilometres along, where the right fork is signposted to Anutz Lake, the left fork to Huson Park.**

This cedar-shaded road twists through second-growth forest. **Follow the signs that direct you to keep right, then left, then make a right turn into the narrower road that leads to the park.** Take it slowly here: this road can surprise you with potholes and bumps. You can park at a small parking area just over 2 kilometres along this road, and plan your walking on the nearby map. Trails lead through the forest down to a karst region, where the subtle pressure from centuries of moving water has carved caves, arches, and bridges in the rock. The pools and waterfalls provide favourite swimming holes for skinny-dipping local residents, and an ideal place to laze away a sunny afternoon.

Little Hustan Caves Park, near the road to Zeballos.

You can retrace your route from the parking area to the road, or continue on along the ever-narrower track, which circles back to the main road. In either case, turn right, and continue on the main road, keeping right at the next fork. Hustan Lake soon shows below the road on the right, with 1,542-metre Pinder Peak dramatic behind the harvested hills ahead.

Some 8 or 9 kilometres (depending on which route you took) from the Little Hustan road, turn left for Zeballos; this turn is signposted. A further 3.4 kilometres along, turn right at the signposted turn for Zeballos, and continue on to Zeballos on Pinder then Zeballos Main, some 33 kilometres to the south. Though this is a public road, watch for industrial traffic.

The Zeballos road skirts Wolfe Lake and Pinder Creek to the right, then follows the Zeballos River to tidewater, between marvellously craggy peaks, including the appropriately named Rugged Mountain, the highest in the area at 1,874 metres. It then slips gently into the tiny town of Zeballos, a three- or four-block main street with one secondary street behind and one main cross street. Zeballos's human history dates back several centuries, from the time the Kyuquot/Checleset people first settled near the head of the inlet.

They have spent far more time here than the man for whom the inlet, river and village are named: Ciriaco Cevallos sailed with Spanish navy captain Alexandro Malaspina, who explored the coast in 1791. Coastal historian John Walbran, by the way, declares that Malaspina was the most romantic figure among European coastal explorers, presumably because he was first feted when he returned to Spain, then imprisoned in a castle for unstated political reasons. He was set free after nine years through the influence of Napoleon, but banished back to his native Italy. His journals were suppressed for almost a hundred years and his role in exploring the coast ignored.

Back to Zeballos, though not to Cevallos, who played no further part on the west-coast stage. Non-natives virtually ignored the area for another century and a half, until wandering prospectors found traces of gold in the nearby hills. In 1929, forty gold claims were staked; by 1936, individual prospectors had given way to mining companies. Two years later, the Spud Valley, Golden Gate, Rey Oro, and White Star mines, plus a handful of others, were producing gold, and Zeballos was a boom town.

Like many another mining rush town, Zeballos's exciting life was short-lived. By 1943, the fixed price of gold, a shortage of miners, and

Zeballos: Yesterday and Today

In the restaurant of the Zeballos Hotel, men in baseball caps and loggers' boots trade stories about the jobs they've worked, up in northern Alberta or the Yukon, tiny camps in northern Ontario, all the isolated places where men mine or log or build dams and roads. Outside, the sun has long since disappeared behind the mountains that close in the few blocks of Zeballos, which lies at the head of a tangle of long narrow inlets that spear east and north from the Pacific.

It's hard to imagine that 1,500 people once lived here, in hotels and bunkhouses built shoulder to shoulder against the mountain, beside the river. How could there have been room on this tiny triangle of flat land for what the *New York Post* described in a February, 1939 article: "the gold-boom town . . . [with] hotels, a hospital, electric light, movies. . . . probably the fastest growing town in Canada?"

The *Post* writer was impressed by the difficulties Zeballos residents overcame: reportedly an inch of rain a day, several feet of snow in the winter, mud, isolation. Some reminders still exist of the days when the mines and the prospecting claims drew hundreds to this isolated pinprick on the west coast.

The Zeballos Hotel began life as the Pioneer Hotel in 1938. It's a nice combination of today and yesterday, where waxed wood tables, swagged curtains, a corner of the bar that replicates the 1930s lobby, and old photos share space with modern mismatched cutlery and cups.

By the door a bulletin board warns of logging road closures and advertises boats for sale.

Tucked in alongside modern houses on Maquinna Street are other '30s relics, clapboarded and false-fronted. But many of Zeballos's original buildings are long gone, most victims of fires that have plagued this community, taking at various times the general store, an apartment building, and, in 1989, the government wharf. Though most maps show that a ferry visits Zeballos, in fact the west-coast supply boat *Uchuck III* calls here only on special occasions and won't return to scheduled service until the wharf is rebuilt.

Down at the remaining docks, kids play and teenagers laugh and listen to music playing on the stereo of a battered car. Once there was a sawmill here; now the area contains two ice plants, a fuel plant, a general store, and the only gas pumps in town.

The Zeballos Board of Trade has published a *Guide to Zeballos*, available from businesses in town.

The Zeballos Hotel.

View at Fair Harbour.

the town's isolated location closed the mines and sent the population plummeting, from 1,500 to 35. Since then, speculators have reopened a mine or two, and an iron mine operated for a time. But Zeballos now lives from logging, though a number of the 1930s buildings still doze on main street.

From Zeballos, a gravel logging road that ranges from very good to adequate leads along inlets and river valleys to Fair Harbour, one-time logging camp, now jumping-off point for Kyuquot Sound and the Checleset Bay Ecological Reserve, traditional territory of the Kyuquot and Checleset native peoples.

To reach Fair Harbour: head north (away from the docks) from the Zeballos Hotel. At about .6 kilometres, turn left over the narrow, picturesque wooden bridge that crosses the Zeballos River. At the stop sign another .7 km along, turn left again. This road, Fair Harbour Mainline, takes you along the western edge of Zeballos Inlet. On your right as you reach the inlet is the Zeballos office of Pacific Forest Products Limited, where you can check road conditions and acquire a map. Also on your right is the Ehattesaht Indian reserve. On your left as you reach the inlet is PFP's dryland log sort and booming area where boom boats hustle around the floating logs. **Keep right up the steep and somewhat rough hill to stay out of the dryland sort.**

For about 5 kilometres, the road—good gravel; watch for logging trucks—curves along the inlet, offering superb views of blue-green water with shadowed mountains behind. It then turns west, to the head of

An old and decaying wharf at Fair Harbour.

The wharf at Fair Harbour.

dog-leg-shaped Little Espinosa Inlet, which almost makes an island out of the peninsula. At around 9 kilometres from Zeballos, the road swings right, across the inlet neck, with more superb views of water and mountains. Note the trailer on a float to the left of the road; floating accommodation towed to its resting place is common on the west coast.

The road—signposted to Fair Harbour at any confusing intersections—crosses a neck of land to the edge of Espinosa Inlet, skirts the inlet and the Ocluje Indian reserve, then cuts cross-country along Espinosa Creek to the Kaouk River, through replanted forests of hemlock, fir, spruce, and cedar. At about 21 kilometres, a sign directs Fair Harbour drivers to the right, onto a road that now gets a little rougher. **Follow Fair Harbour Main through a forested, mountain-**

girt valley, keeping left across a bridge at 26 kilometres (signposted; Kaouk Main is to your right).

The country the road traverses now changes character, from rough and rugged to gentle valley territory, where alders and evergreens over-reach the road. **The inlet head is at about 34.6 kilometres; follow the signs across two bridges that span the marshy land at the head of Fair Harbour, to a campsite, parking lot, and dock about a kilometre farther on.**

There are few deep and protected anchorages along the wild west coast of Vancouver Island. Fair Harbour is so-named because it's one of the few. Walk down to the dock from the wide flat area that once housed a logging camp, and you'll see its charm. Small rockfish and minnows swarm in deep, clear, green water; mussels, barnacles, and bright purple starfish cling to the dock pilings. Beyond the remains of an old dock to the east, herons, kingfishers, ducks, crows, and gulls swoop or settle on the water.

It's such a quiet idyllic scene that the several dozen cars and trucks usually in the parking lot come as a surprise. Though Fair Harbour is no longer a logging camp—its houses were moved to Zeballos in 1970, when the logging road joined the two—it is still busy. Water taxis carry people to fish farms along the inlet, to isolated logging camps, and to Kyuquot, headquarters of the Kyuquot Indian band. Kayakers and other boaters launch here for an exploration of the beautiful and protected waters, some going as far as the Brooks Peninsula provincial wilderness recreation area to the northwest.

The journey is increasingly attractive to modern-day explorers. The rectangular Brooks Peninsula is an oddity. The only part of Vancouver Island to escape glaciation, it is home to plant species not found else-where. By 1900, the sea otter was extinct on the west coast, exterminated by voracious fur traders. Some twenty-five years ago, Alaskan otters were transplanted to Checleset Bay, between Kyuquot and the Brooks Peninsula, where the species is re-establishing itself.

Return along the Fair Harbour Mainline to Zeballos Inlet, and continue straight on past the Zeballos turn to rejoin the Zeballos Mainline.

To return to the tour starting point, continue straight on the Zeballos road back to the highway, some 43 kilometres from Zeballos. At Highway 19, turn left for Port McNeill and north island points, right to return towards Campbell River.

PORT MCNEILL TO PORT ALICE AND BACK

This tour provides a rare north island opportunity to go somewhere on a paved road, though more than half of the route reverts to gravel logging roads. It demonstrates just how deeply Pacific inlets cut into northern Vancouver Island, for it touches Pacific tidewater little more than an hour by vehicle from the waters of Queen Charlotte and Broughton straits that run between the island and the mainland. It skirts or parallels long narrow lakes that lie in the deep valleys of the mountain chain, runs briefly beside a Pacific inlet, twists with mountain rivers beside limestone formations, and cuts across country past freshwater lakes known for their fishing. If you just go to Port Alice and back, this is a half-day trip. If you complete the full circle, you should allow a day, and take with you food, drink, and the usual emergency supplies.

The first half of the tour is suitable for any vehicle and most drivers. From Port Alice on, you can choose a logging road route that is equally suitable for most vehicles and drivers, or you can take a more scenic but somewhat more difficult route, with one stretch of several hundred metres that must be taken at a snail's pace. Much of the route is good at any time—barring, snow, ice, or slush. Check at Jeune Landing for conditions on the route around the south end of Victoria Lake, and also to determine if there is active logging on any part of the route.

An alternate route side trip to Mahatta River can apparently be done in a two-wheel-drive vehicle—I confess I have not attempted it, but have been told it is probably best attempted in a high-clearance vehicle by drivers who are not concerned about narrow roads and steep drop-offs.

Before You Go

Western Forest Products North Island logging road and recreation guide and MacMillan Bloedel's Port Hardy/Port McNeill map are essential companions. Enquire locally for conditions past Port Alice. Western Forest Products at Jeune Landing can advise you about conditions, give you a map that covers the Mahatta River-Victoria Lake area, and let you know if roads are closed or not recommended because of active logging. MacMillan Bloedel in Port McNeill can advise you about conditions on the road from Alice Lake back to Port McNeill.

☙ ☙ ☙

The tour begins at Port McNeill. **Follow Broughton Street north from Port McNeill's waterfront onto Beach Drive. This street becomes a gravel road as you leave town. Stay left at the first Y in the road, then take the first right. Continue to a stop sign, and turn left onto Rupert Main.** Rupert Main takes you to a campsite, picnic site, and boat launch. Nearby is a salt marsh with trails from Rupert Main to wildlife viewing points in the marsh. **Continue on Rupert Main, keeping left at a Y in the road approximately 6 kilometres from the salt marsh, and you will intersect Highway 19 another 2 kilometres along. Turn left, then make an immediate right onto the road signposted to Port Alice.**

This paved road winds through forest and mountains 33 kilometres to Port Alice. A public road, it is open to all traffic at all times. The trip to Port Alice and back makes a pleasant afternoon's excursion if you're not in the mood for more gravel and dust.

Just after the turn-off, Beaver Lake appears on the right, with picnic tables and swimming. On the left is the entrance to the Beaver Lake Trail, through a demonstration forest with information signs. Continue southwest, past the entrance to a golf course, until you cross the Marble River just under 15 kilometres from the highway. Turn right, to meander down through fine old cedar trees to the Marble River, a camp and picnic site with hiking trails down to and along the river. Turn left for the Alice Lake boat launch and for a fish hatchery that offers tours.

Back on the road, Alice Lake appears on the left. Both Port Alice and the lake are named for Alice Whalen, mother of the two men who founded the pulp and paper company that built a mill on the shores of Neroutsos Inlet in 1917. Alice Lake stretches, long and narrow, southwest for some 15 kilometres; it's a local favourite for fishing, canoeing, and swimming.

A left turn 28 kilometres from the highway is signposted to Mount Waddington Regional District's Link River campsite, so-named because the river links Alice Lake with longer and equally narrow Victoria Lake. Thirty-two kilometres from the highway, a road leads right into Jeune Landing, once the major community in the area and still the site of logging company offices, and 3 kilometres to the north, the Quatsino dryland timber sort. The name Jeune ties together much history on Vancouver Island. The Jeune brothers who arrived in Victoria in gold-rush days were Channel Islanders who set up a sail-making business. As sons and then grandsons joined the business, it expanded to making almost anything of canvas, including tents and tarpaulins, and

Looking out into the fog on Victoria Lake.

shipping them to points such as this. Jeune Brothers still sells tents and other outdoor gear in Victoria.

Half a kilometre along, the main road enters the village of Port Alice. Instant communities are a commonplace in British Columbia, where seekers after riches or jobs quickly follow mineral finds or the establishment of mill or mine. Port Alice was the first official instant municipality, incorporated in 1965, before either Port Hardy or Port McNeill. Almost fifty years earlier, millworkers moved into dwellings at a townsite close to the pulp mill that opened in 1918, south of the present town. After Rayonier Inc. acquired a major interest in the mill in 1952, the company built a new townsite in 1965, in the present location. Now, some 2,000 people, most firmly linked to logging or the mill, live at Port Alice.

Continue through Port Alice, past a civic boat launch and picnic site on your right. Note warning signs that indicate roads around the inlet are subject to slides in heavy rain. Just over 5 kilometres from the town centre, the pulp mill appears below and on your right, beside the inlet. **Keep left where the road forks; the right fork enters the mill. Two hundred metres farther on, you have a choice.**

Optional: keep right for an adventuresome journey around the inlet, switchbacking up mountainsides and across logged hillsides, to the tiny logging camp at Mahatta River on Quatsino Sound, or on to Klaskino Inlet and views of the open Pacific. We have not yet attempted this route, and it isn't described here. If you choose to drive it, check beforehand with Western Forest Products to make sure the road is open to non-logging traffic, and take with you the WFP map or the MacMillan Bloedel map that covers this area. Even if you don't want to make the several-hour journey to the coast, you can follow Marine Drive around the inlet head and up the switchbacks for good views—provided the inlet isn't swathed in the cottonwool fog that often blankets the area.

To follow the main route, keep left just past the Port Alice pulp mill to drive along Victoria Lake and complete a circle tour back to Port McNeill. Just over 3 kilometres from the mill, you'll reach an intersection. Continue down the hill for a good view of Victoria Lake, particularly attractive on mornings when fog and low cloud sift in up the Marble River valley from the Pacific. Return up the hill, and it's decision time.

• **Option 1** involves a challenging but pretty trip high above Victoria Lake, then down across the river at the head of the lake, then up the lake's other shore. Logging was going on around the south end of Victoria Lake in 1996, so the road may be closed weekdays, and used by logging trucks and large trucks hauling limestone at any time. WFP has improved these roads around the southern end of the lake, making the trip easier, but the road is busier than it used to be.

If you want to take this southern route, turn south on Port Alice Main (left if you're coming up the hill from the lake, right if you're coming from Port Alice), then keep left 200 metres later. Follow this road high above the lake until you see the marker that reads PA Main 28. This is a beautiful road in the sunshine, though not highly recommended in the rain, running between cliffs that tower above the lake far below. **Go down the hill after the PA Main 28 marker, and look for a road on your left: it's easy to miss. Turn left.** This road is at the end of the lake, so if you start climbing again and can no longer see the lake below, make a U-turn: you're on a dead-end logging road.

The road around the end of the lake was a narrow, rocky, bumpy spur when we tried it, and required slow and careful driving for a few hundred metres. Western Forest Products say they have now improved the road.

Continue across the bridge over the Marble River, then keep left, back up the east side of the lake, on Victoria Lake Main.

The Coastal Western Hemlock Zone

Along the Spruce Bay old-growth trail, Sitka spruce spear 50 metres into the air, dwarfing the western hemlock beside the earlier part of the trail. Spreading blueberry plants hug the ground; sword ferns fringe the areas where some light penetrates the forest canopy.

This forest provides a glimpse of the plants and trees of the Coastal Western Hemlock Zone, a biogeoclimatic region that covers almost all of Vancouver Island, excluding only the high mountains of the island spine and the small Douglas-fir zone at the southeast tip.

As the name indicates, western hemlock is the dominant tree species in the region. Floppy-topped, with flat, short needles, and tiny cones that occur in great numbers, hemlocks can grow in the deep shade created by the taller Douglas-firs and Sitka spruce. That ability gives hemlock a great advantage in the island forest, for both Douglas-fir and spruce need light and open space to grow.

If you look around at the forest floor of a coastal forest, it is hemlock seedlings that you will see, sprouting from rotting logs, popping up from debris. When the other coniferous species die in old age, the hemlocks that grew in their shade replace them. Only fire, wind, flood, or logging results in the light and open space that encourage Douglas-fir and Sitka spruce.

Sitka spruce thrive in the wet weather and the salt spray of the west coast. Along with Douglas-fir and western red cedar, it is the giant of the area, growing as tall as 60 metres in just a hundred years, adding as much as 30 centimetres to its diameter every thirty to thirty-five years.

Blueberries, huckleberries, ferns, mosses, and salal also grow in this zone, providing a chaotic understorey wherever the forest floor is exposed to light.

The best examples of old-growth forest in this zone can be seen at Carmanah and at Cape Scott.

Two kilometres past a bridge near the VL 23 milepost, turn left into the Spruce Bay Recreation Area. Always a nice place to stop, attracting locals for the weekend or longer, Spruce Bay is now a must-visit: a kilometre-long trail winds through old growth that is a rare sight anywhere within driving range, where most areas have been logged and replanted with cedar, balsam, hemlock, Douglas-fir, and Sitka spruce. In this old-growth area, majestic Sitka spruce 50 and more metres high, 3 metres around, with the occasional cedar, provide a glimpse of what the best growing sites in this area must have looked like a hundred—or even fifty—years ago. The trail comes out on Victoria Lake Main, but it's far more pleasant to retrace your steps through the forest than to walk back down the road and into the recreation area. Black bears frequent this area, so you might want to talk loudly as you walk through the woods.

Return to Victoria Lake Main and continue north. The road provides glimpses of the lake; trucks parked at various places along the road indicate squatters' houses hidden in the bush. A long winding hill brings you down to the end of the lake and a T-junction. **Turn right at this road, Southeast Main.**

• **Option 2 also starts 3 kilometres from the Port Alice mill, at the intersection overlooking the lake. This route is an easier path that winds around the north end of the lake to join Southeast Main. To follow this route, turn north and follow the road to the north end of Victoria Lake. Turn right at the intersection with Southeast Main, then turn right again at Victoria Lake Main to reach the Spruce Bay campsite and old-growth trail described above.**

Return to Southeast Main at the north end of Victoria Lake and turn right, away from Port Alice. This wide, good gravel road acquires various names as it continues on. Stay on the main road which is here surfaced with white gravel made from crushed limestone. **About 5 kilometres along, a sign points left towards the Eternal Fountain.** Though it appears in all the tourist brochures, you may find this limestone formation a bit of an anti-climax. The Eternal Fountain is the result of water eroding limestone: a stream falls over a rock lip, then turns back in the direction it came to disappear under itself. **To reach the fountain, turn left and cross the new bridge. Just across the bridge turn right.** This turn may be signposted. Grouse scare up under your tires on this narrow, overgrown track, but it's quite passable. **Keep right with the sign about 1.8 kilometres along, then park another hundred metres along, and walk down to the river on your right.**

Return to the main road and continue east. This road is signposted to the Devil's Bath and Port McNeill. **About 5 kilometres along, a small sign points left towards the Devil's Bath.** You can park off the road and walk to the lip of a second geological formation of eroded limestone, this one a more interesting deep pool below white limestone walls.

Continue on through young cedar along a good road. About 3.5 kilometres from the Devil's Bath, keep left; the right fork goes to Trasco on Branch 909. Drive down a long winding hill, then keep right over a bridge across Craft Creek. Though the workings are some distance from the road, signs along here indicate where mines were once located.

About 6 kilometres from Devil's Bath, Benson Lake, a pretty body of water with lake access and boat launch, appears on your

left. **Continue past mountain views and along the Benson River on your left a further 6 kilometres. Then turn left, on a road signposted to Port McNeill. Straight on takes you to Atluck Lake and a long trip to Zeballos (see Tour 16).**

The left turn across the bridge takes you past an access to a walking trail along Trout Lake. Note that milepost signs have changed here, to the red and white that indicates MacMillan Bloedel logging roads. The road from here on is wide and better than the average back road.

Cross a second bridge, this one across the Raging River (not too raging at the end of a dry summer), then keep left where the road forks about 800 metres from the bridge. You are now on Benson Main, which will lead you back to Port McNeill, past a series of small lakes that attract fishers and boaters. Iron Lake, probably named for its reddish colour, is first on the left. Next comes Maynard Lake, the largest of the roadside lakes, with a recreation site and boat launch, followed about 6.5 kilometres later by Three Isle Lake, then Angler Lake.

Keogh Lake is the first large lake on the right. Four kilometres past Keogh Lake, an acute right leads to Cluxewe Lake and the starting point of a hiking trail.

Continue straight on, past a left turn to O'Connor Lake Recreation Site, and reach the highway at a stop sign. Cross the highway to see the world's biggest burl, at the entrance to MacBlo's Port McNeill headquarters. **Continue straight ahead,** past the burl; this logging road will bring you out in the centre of Port McNeill.

TOUR 18 HOLBERG, WINTER HARBOUR, AND SAN JOSEF BAY

This is the most interesting of the north island tours. It packs visits to three ocean inlets into a remarkably short distance, adds an option for a fourth inlet, and provides opportunities for walks through rainforest and along wave-swept beaches. The tour takes you to a fishing port, a logging town, a heritage garden, and the beginning of the famed Cape Scott trail. It's a good day's journey, with many worthwhile stops. If you have camping gear, the trip can occupy several days; if not, you'll have to return to town for overnight stays. There are some commercial facilities at Holberg and Winter Harbour, but they keep irregular hours.

The trip is suitable for most cars and drivers who are at home with gravel roads that contain the occasional rough or overgrown section. Good weather provides the best conditions and views, though, like any gravel roads, these can be dusty. The roads should still be passable in wet weather but snow would pose a problem. The roads are well signposted and for the most part well maintained. Take the usual emergency supplies for logging road travel. If you venture away from the main gravel roads, you should be prepared for industrial traffic, road closures, and unexpected changes in road surface and condition.

But the main roads provide enough excitement and interest for most people. Along the way are forest, rivers and lakes; a busy fishing village and a sleepy town; a good pub with a view of the inlet; and excellent forest-to-beach walking trails that take from twenty minutes to two hours.

Before You Go

You do need to take a map with you here. Almost any map of the north island will show you the main roads. For more detail and up-to-date logging road routes, get Western Forest Products *Visitors' Guide to North ern Vancouver Island*, available at infocentres and from WFP offices in Port McNeill, Port Alice, Holberg, Coal Harbour, and Winter Harbour.

ⓐ ⓐ ⓐ

The tour begins at the junction of Highway 19 and the Holberg/Cape Scott Road about 2 kilometres south of Port Hardy, 200 metres north of the Coal Harbour turn-off. **Turn west on the Holberg Road (left if you are heading towards Port Hardy, right if you are heading south).** Just 2.5 kilometres along, the road becomes gravel. At 7.2 kilometres, a side road leads to Georgie Lake, with a campsite and boat launch. Continue past cedar and floppy-topped hemlock just over 6 kilometres to Kains Lake, and keep an eye out for the Shoe Tree on your left.

Holberg resident Tracey Anonson was living in Holberg in 1988 and bored to tears with the featureless road between Holberg and Port Hardy, a road Holberg residents had to drive all too often to get groceries or reach appointments in town. She determined that something had to be done to liven up the trip. In the Ontario town where she had lived, some-one had started a shoe tree, where people nailed old shoes to a tree trunk. She and a logger friend chose a likely looking cedar snag about 20 metres high beside Kains Lake; she nailed on a pair of her son's dead sneakers, and the Holberg Road shoe tree was established.

Even Anonson is astonished at the tree's success. Several hundred pairs of running shoes, baby shoes, pumps, hiking boots, rubber boots, are nailed to every centimetre on the lower part of the tree, and someone with climbing gear and a sense of humour has placed hiking boots high on the snag, climbing to the top. Regrettably, someone has liberated the parody poem once in place: "Give me your worn, your torn;" it ran, "Your decrepit sneakers yearning to breathe free,/ The wretched refuse of your active feet,/ Send these, the loved and discarded to me." Though that sign is gone, others posted by travellers from places as distant as France and Japan remain among the tattered soles and uppers.

Just over 9 kilometres from the shoe tree, a road leads to the right, to the eastern end of Nahwitti Lake. Two more roads along the length of the lake lead to picnic and camp sites in the forest and to boat launches. **Past Nahwitti Lake, signposts point Holberg and Cape Scott travellers to the left, then left again 4 kilometres farther on.** Across a bridge some 11 kilometres from Nahwitti Lake, a fake outhouse has been painted onto a tall tree stump by the side of the road. Local legend has it that the outhouse was created in honour of a one-time Holberg resident who was famous for always having to stop at least once on the road from Holberg to Port Hardy. Passersby with a different sense of humour have sent gun blasts into the seated figure painted behind the outhouse door. The sign that warns you that 12 whistles don't mean lunchtime suggests that some neophyte backroaders need to brush up on their logging-road etiquette, at least to the extent of knowing that 12 whistles signal imminent blasting, usually for road construction.

About 4 kilometres past the outhouse, a long hill leads down into Holberg. Once the site of what was said to be the world's largest float camp, Holberg is now firmly ashore, though considerably smaller than it used to be. The Holberg armed forces base that once housed 500 people is all but deserted today, and the town's population has dropped to about 200.

The road swings onto pavement through the town, past a store and the lone pub on this west-coast road. Gone are the days when a logging town centred on a beer parlour that served one brand of draft and food was measured in pickled eggs and pepperoni. The Holberg pub, The Scarlet Ibis, looks out over the inlet, serves several draft beers including a natural ale, is known for its good food, and is as likely to be filled with tired Cape Scott hikers as with burly loggers.

From Holberg, you can proceed to Winter Harbour and/or Cape Scott Provincial Park, or, if you feel more adventuresome, you can explore a side trip over relatively new logging roads to Koprino Inlet.

Optional: to make the Koprino Inlet trip (a route we have not driven) pick up a WFP map at the Holberg WFP office and check on whether the road is open and/or recommended. This is apparently a scenic drive; Western Forest Products employees at Holberg suggest it's a good side trip for those who don't mind roads that can be rough.

• For Koprino Inlet, keep left through the logging company yards onto South Main, then turn left just outside town to drive along Holberg Inlet's south shore. Watch for logging traffic here: trucks bring timber from the surrounding area to the log dump on the inlet. About 3.5 kilometres from town, keep straight ahead on Lake Main, then veer right on Southeast Main in another 1.5 kilometres. Southeast Main becomes Koprino Main and leads to a campsite, boat launch, and dock at Koprino Harbour on Quatsino Sound.

When you return towards Holberg, the map may tempt you to cut across country on South Main to the Winter Harbour road. WFP staff suggest you forego the shortcut: logging traffic can be heavy on this narrow, winding road that offers little in the way of pleasant views. Return, instead to Holberg, and take the regular route to Winter Harbour.

• To travel to Winter Harbour, stay on the pavement through Holberg, then turn left where the road is signposted to Winter Harbour and Cape Scott, just past the WFP office. This is the red road on the WFP map; it joins up with San Josef Main. A kilometre along, you pass the Cordy Creek Hatchery. Keep left over the bridge, and about 4 kilometres along, you'll see a straight-faced warning sign for elephants crossing. Once upon a time, the Elephant Crossing sign was gaudier, with pink and red elephants, leading to speculation that the name came not from the giant logging trucks that use the road but from visions in the heads of loggers who imbibed too much.

Keep straight on at the stop sign (a right turn takes you to San Josef Bay and Cape Scott park). This road, which also leads to the former CFB base, is less used than it was when the base was flourishing. About 9 kilometres from Holberg, the road intersects the Winter Harbour road. Straight on leads to a locked gate that guards the old base location; **turn left for Winter Harbour.**

The road to Winter Harbour cuts through rounded hills and mingled forest and clear-cut, replanted land. All the main intersections are signposted; **keep right at about 15 kilometres from town, keep right again at 25.7 kilometres (left leads to a logging camp); then continue straight on a kilometre later.** West Main leads to the right here through an active logging area to the Grant Bay hiking trail, a strenuous slog through difficult territory to an attractive cove facing the open Pacific.

The Winter Harbour road gets a little rougher now that it emerges from active logging areas to run below a canopy of trees. **Follow the signs (keep left at 28.3 kilometres, keep right at 28.9 kilometres)** and you'll reach Kwaksiskah Regional Park on your left as the road

The famed Elephant Crossing sign near Holberg.

curves right, a beautiful camp and picnic site with covered tables and fire grates looking out over Winter Harbour and west to Forward Inlet. A sign reminds us of the long human history on this coast: broad cedar stumps are left from ancient cedars the Kwakwaka'wakw used to make dugout canoes a century and more ago. The canoe was shaped from the log by using a combination of fire and adze and chisel work. Water was poured into the hollowed-out interior, and brought to a boil as hot stones were added. Mats kept the steam in; when the wood had softened sufficiently, the canoe makers forced in thwarts to spread the sides.

A few hundred metres past the park, the road enters the community of Winter Harbour. You have already bypassed what used to be known as Downtown Winter Harbour—the logging camp 4 kilometres back; the fishing village is Uptown Winter Harbour. Park opposite the dock (watch for restricted parking signs) to explore the village on foot. You'll meet a lot of yachters and other boaters here: the Winter Harbour store houses the only liquor outlet on the west coast north of Zeballos (then again, maybe they're just picking up food supplies).

Winter Harbour takes its name from the refuge it provides from winter storms in the open Pacific. A glance at the map shows that it's the closest safe harbour for any ship off the north island's west coast. If you park near the dock, you can stroll past fish boats and yachts, walk a short boardwalk to the general store, or chat to lounging fishers. Hard though

The Tuna Fleet at Winter Harbour

It's line-up time down at the pay phones by the Winter Harbour dock: one of the phones is out of order, and everyone wants to phone home today. But the fishers off the tuna boats take it all in their stride. When you've been at sea for weeks, or even months, an additional half-hour doesn't seem to mean too much.

Visit Winter Harbour in the fall, and you'll find it busy. Captains and crew are dinghying down to Kwaksiskah Park for an afternoon barbecue, everyone—even back-roaders—invited; or hanging out at the store, buying provisions or contributing to the wall of fishboat photos. But these fishers and fish-boats are a little different from the ones British Columbians usually see at Victoria or any of the ports along the coast of Vancouver Island. This is the offshore tuna fleet, putting in to a Canadian port after months in other waters.

In a bad year—which most years are now that the salmon are depleted off the B.C. coast—you'll see Canadian fishboats, rerigged with lines and hooks to catch tuna: the five- to six-kilogram fish known as schoolers, up to fish of ten kilos and more. But most tuna boats are American, on an offshore odyssey that takes them thousands of kilometres back and forth across the Pacific.

They fish for albacore, a white-fleshed fish that commands the best prices and is said to be the best of the tuna. They start from the American west coast, most from California, in April, motoring down to warmer waters where the albacore are, near Hawaii, or Midway, or Tahiti. Once at sea, they stay at sea for weeks, unloading to a roving fish packer that also refuels and resupplies them. But heaven help them if the season has been bad: the mother boat supplies fuel on a strict gallons-of-gas to tons-of-catch ratio. Then the packer leaves, the catch in its holds destined for a fish plant in American Samoa.

The tuna fishers come north with the warm water and the tuna. By September, they crowd into the docks at Winter Harbour, as some of them have for twenty-five years. There they renew acquaintance with old friends, pick up supplies, trade stories with the locals, and phone home or to marine supply depots that just may have the parts they need. Then it's off again, back to open water and their deep-sea fishing.

The fishing fleet ties up at Winter Harbour.

it is to imagine the scene now, in the 1970s, so many people—several thousand, it's estimated—came to Winter Harbour for an annual jazz festival that locals grew tired of the problems the big crowds caused and ended the event.

Walk along the main road from the dock towards the store and you'll see a flight of wooden stairs leading into the forest. This ten-minute hike through old-growth spruce and balsam leads to a beach on Forward Inlet. After the bustle of Winter Harbour, and the constant sound of a compressor on the docks, the silence and solitude just around the corner seem remarkable.

Retrace your route back towards Holberg. At about 19 kilometres from Winter Harbour, keep straight on to San Josef Bay (on your way to Winter Harbour, you turned left at the stop sign at this intersection). This disused logging road quickly narrows; grass grows at the road centre, and bear scat indicates that bears appreciate the absence of logging trucks. Grouse rise under your wheels and water lilies grow in a marshy area alongside the road. This road demands caution, as sharp rocks protrude, but it is rewarding, both because it's attractive and because you may see wildlife here that you rarely see on more travelled roads.

About 3 kilometres from the intersection, keep left on a wide, better-maintained logging road. A kilometre farther on, turn left on San Josef Main, which will take you to the Cape Scott area a half-hour's drive away.

The road is well signposted from here to Cape Scott park. Three kilometres along, keep left on San Josef Main where Stranby Main branches to your right. About 1.3 kilometres beyond Stranby Main, an almost illegible stop of interest sign half-hidden in the bushes on your right commemorates a wagon road built across country in 1912 to the home of a settler near here.

Just beyond the sign, the road crosses the San Juan River, then continues through a stand of timber that regenerated naturally here after a hurricane blew down much of the forest in 1906. **Keep straight on at the next two intersections, both signposted,** though if you are in the mood for an energetic side trip, you could turn left at the second intersection, on Ronning Main, signposted for Raft Cove Provincial Park 12 kilometres away.

Declared a park in 1992, Raft Cove faces the open Pacific and is billed as one of the most rugged and spectacular on the island coast. Original

The Cape Scott Settlers and Ronning's Garden

British Columbia has been home to many a failed Utopia, and the northwest tip of Vancouver Island has its own story of dreams and disappointment. At the turn of the century, Danish immigrants working as fishermen landed near Cape Scott, named more than a hundred years before for David Scott, a Bombay merchant who had outfitted a trading expedition to the northwest coast.

They convinced other Danish immigrants that the distant region could be a promised land. By 1900, some seventy-five families were homesteading on land near Cape Scott, in the San Josef Valley and east. But this heavily forested, stormy land was not kind to settlers, and by 1909, most had left behind their homes, a school, a sawmill, and other community buildings. Then, a second, equally short-lived wave of settlement began. When the young men left to fight in World War I, the farms were soon abandoned and the forests took over once more. Even now, few live west or north of Holberg.

Two who do have taken it upon themselves to restore an old settler's dream. Ron and Julia Moe live on the land homesteaded by Bernt Ronning from 1910 to the 1960s. On two hectares of land he cleared, Ronning planted seeds and cuttings he ordered from far distant sources, and his

Monkey puzzle trees at Ronning's Garden.

garden became that cliché, an oasis in the wilderness.

The Moes have tried to re-establish that garden. They have made visible and labelled the old monkey puzzle trees that once stood sentry outside Ronning's house, bamboo and golden yew, Portuguese laurel and scarlet hawthorn, among many other trees.

The Ronning Garden is beside the old wagon road promised as an access road for the Cape Scott settlers. The promise was not kept: the wagon road ended not far past Ronning's homestead. To reach the garden, walk along the narrow track that alone remains of the unfinished road.

The trail to San Josef Bay, Cape Scott Provincial Park.

trails from parking lot to beach were difficult and challenging, but in 1995, a new road was being built closer to the water, eliminating the most difficult part of the hike.

Continue along the road to San Josef. Cross the San Juan River again, and keep an eye out for a small sign that indicates a lane on the right that leads to Ronning's Garden. **Turn right and park at a clearing 200 metres along, just past a narrow track blocked by stones. The track leads to the garden.**

Return to the San Josef road and continue west, through a clear-cut that was replanted in 1993. **Keep straight on about 4 kilometres from the garden turn, then keep left another 800 metres ahead;** both turns are signposted for Cape Scott. A left turn another 600 metres down the road leads you to the San Josef Recreation Area, a pleasant campsite amid tall balsam and spruce, where Cape Scott hikers can catch their breath after the strenuous hike. **Continue along the San**

San Josef Bay, Cape Scott Provincial Park.

Josef road past the left turn to a boat launch on the San Josef River
to the parking lot at the trailheads for San Josef Bay and Cape
Scott.

Though the trail to Cape Scott, on the northwest tip of the island,
promises fine old-growth forest and magnificent views of wind and wave-
swept beaches, it is a two-day, strenuous hike to the cape and return, on
a trail that can be very muddy and difficult. Day hikers turn instead to
the trail to San Josef Bay, a forty-five-minute hike through rainforest, most
of it quite easy, on boardwalks or a chip trail.

The walk is worthwhile. A half-hour's hiking through the forest of
hemlock, fir, and cedar brings you to your first glimpse of San Josef Bay,
a long, deep curve from open ocean to the mouth of the San Juan River.
As you come down towards the water, you can cut off on trails that lead
to the left, to walk the beach, or you can continue to the camp and picnic
site beside a wide stretch of sand that looks out to the ocean.

**Return to the parking lot, and retrace your road route to
Holberg, and Port Hardy.**

 **HEADING SOUTH**

A number of shorter side trips are possible on paved or
gravel logging roads that loop off from the main north
island highway. One such leads to the community of
Coal Harbour, another through Telegraph Cove, built mostly out over
the water on pilings supported by boardwalks. Then, from Woss, south
of Nimpkish Lake, you can follow what was once the only land route to
the north island, a gravel logging road that follows the Nimpkish Valley
southeast almost along the middle of the island, then crosses the height
of land to follow streams and rivers that flow towards the Pacific. This
road rejoins a paved highway at Gold River, for a 90-kilometre return
through scenic territory to Campbell River.

Before You Go

Collect all the logging-company maps you can find for these routes, since
they cross through the leases of different companies. MacMillan Bloedel's
*Recreation and Logging Road Guide to Forestlands of Northern Vancouver Is-
land: Port McNeill/Port Hardy* covers the Telegraph Cove-Bonanza Lake
route. Canadian Forest Products produces a map and guide to the
Nimpkish Valley area; though accurate, it is, unfortunately, extremely difficult to read. All the usual logging road cautions apply on these two

routes: no services en route, gravel roads, conditions that might have changed since this book was written. Take the usual emergency supplies, plus food and drink.

I Port Hardy to Coal Harbour

This half-hour side trip on a paved road is good in all weathers, for all manner of vehicles and drivers, and for cyclists. **From Highway 19 south of Port Hardy, turn west on the road signposted for Coal Harbour, opposite Hardy Bay Road.** Just a kilometre from the highway, Byng Road loops to the left, past Quatse River Hatchery. Turn here to tour the salmon hatchery, and to follow nature trails along the Quatse River, with information posted on salmonid life cycles and local flora and fauna.

Continue west on Coal Harbour Road. About 8.3 kilometres from the highway, turn left for the Island Copper Mine. This huge open-pit mine, scheduled to close in 1995, is visible from an observation deck above the pit.

Continue west. The Quatsino First Nations territory is about 5 kilometres farther along; look for whale carvings and the Quattisme Hall on your right. At about 13.7 kilometres from the highway, you cross Coal Harbour Main, a rough and active logging road that leads (to the right) to good views along Holberg Inlet. The main road then curves into downtown Coal Harbour.

Though the tourist literature still describes Coal Harbour as "quaint," it has in fact become the best-looking suburb of Port Hardy. Straight ahead is the harbour and dock, where fishboats share space with tugs, sailboats, yachts, and motor boats. Water taxis leave from the wharf for Quatsino, 14 kilometres away by sea, where visitors find a hamlet accessible only by water, with an 1896 church and a 1912 hotel renovated as a guest house. On the sea side of the Coal Harbour street that parallels the water north of the dock stand some of the nicest houses in the area, looking out over Holberg Inlet.

Coal Harbour takes its name from poor-quality coal deposits discovered in the 1880s and briefly mined. But Coal Harbour's real boom times came between 1940 and 1967. From 1941 to 1948, the Royal Canadian Air Force maintained a seaplane base and reconnaissance station here, flying patrol missions along the coast. A flying boat hangar remains near the harbour.

From 1947 till 1967, Coal Harbour was a whaling station, where whalers brought their leviathans for processing. The jawbone from a blue whale stands more than 6 metres tall beside the street to the north of the harbour, together with a plaque that honours those who served on the RCAF base.

Return via the paved road to Port Hardy. Check road restrictions for active logging: you may also be able to return via the road that leads to Island Copper Mine along the end of Rupert Inlet to Port Hardy Main and the Port Alice Road. Consult the Western Forest Products area visitors' map for various possible routes.

II Port McNeill to Telegraph Cove, Bonanza Lake and Nimpkish Lake

This tour follows a paved and public gravel road 16 kilometres to Telegraph Cove, a boardwalk community founded on fishing and forestry and now better known as a base for whale watching. It then continues south on gravel roads some 40 kilometres past lakes and through second-growth forest, to rejoin Highway 19 south of Nimpkish Lake. The paved road is suitable in all weathers for all vehicles and drivers; the gravel logging road is best in good weather, for drivers and vehicles that can handle a reasonably good logging road.

✠ ✠ ✠

From the Port McNeill intersection on the Island Highway, drive south 7 kilometres and turn left at the road signposted for Telegraph Cove. Just a hundred metres off the highway, turn left for the North Island Forestry Centre, where you can get back-road maps and

The boardwalk at Telegraph Cove.

information on the north island, or arrange for a forest tour sponsored by one of the five major companies active on the north island. The tours, which run about five hours each, visit logging camps, see log-handling equipment, travel on a logging railway behind a steam locomotive, visit fish hatcheries, and/or present nature walks and boat rides.

Continue on the Telegraph Cove Road. About 11 kilometres from the highway, keep left towards Telegraph Cove; just beyond this fork, you'll cross the Kokish River. Look upstream to see an old railway trestle still used by the logging railway that carries timber from logging operations to the log sort at Beaver Cove. You'll cross these railway tracks half a kilometre along, then continue along the main road past the railway tracks, log booms, and log sort at Beaver Cove.

The road ends at Telegraph Cove, beyond Beaver Cove. The telegraph line built in 1911–12 between Campbell River and the north island—the only communications link between the two—ended at Telegraph Cove. The land rises sharply from the waterfront here, and like many another coastal outpost, the new community was built mainly on pilings and floats extended over the water. Unlike many other towns, Telegraph Cove has been preserved. Its neatly painted houses, each with a sign describing its original use and inhabitants, the boardwalk, the flower boxes, benches, and lights, are the result of a major restoration project. The signs note the activities of Japanese and other residents, who owned or worked at a chum salmon saltery and a small sawmill where boxes for the salmon were made.

Those days are gone. Telegraph Cove is now known world-wide as the base for whale-watching expeditions down Johnstone Strait to Robson Bight, an ecological reserve where orcas rub on the beaches at the mouth of the Tsitika River, or offshore, where wandering pods of whales gather.

Turn back along the road you came in on, and drive about 2 kilometres to a left fork in the road. Keep left for Bonanza Lake. This moderately pleasant but unexciting road winds about 42 kilometres above Ida and Bonanza lakes to Steele Creek and the north island highway.

About 11 kilometres along this road, just past a bridge over the Kokish River, a spur road branches right, to a campsite back across the river at the head of Ida Lake. **Continue along the logging road,** through reforested hillsides and along swampy areas. A few kilometres beyond Ida Lake, Bonanza Lake appears below, on the right. Several stories explain Bonanza's name: you can choose the one you like. The lake and river are named either for high-grade copper ore discovered in the 1920s, or for the stands of timber around the lake. Spur roads lead to campsites at each end of the lake: a small site beside the marshy area at the lake's north end, and a larger, more heavily used site with mature second-growth cedar and hemlock and a sandy beach at the south end. Along the way, you may see limestone blocks cut and numbered from a limestone quarry near the road. A whitish, comparatively soft sedimentary rock made of calcium carbonate, limestone is a feature of the area's geology, more interesting perhaps in the eroded limestone formations off the Zeballos road and near Port Alice.

Keep right where the road forks about 28.4 kilometres from the beginning of the logging road, through a logging yard, and across the Bonanza River. You'll pass Whistle Corner, its name presumably a warning to trucks on the road, then continue up the river valley. About 2.5 kilometres past Whistle Corner is a gravel pit used as a swimming hole; a further 1.5 kilometres along is a trail that leads to Steele Lake.

Continue on the main road, keeping right where the left turn is marked as Markusen Road. About 1.5 kilometres farther on, you'll reach Highway 19; turn right for Port McNeill, left for down-island points. To the right just before you reach the highway is a railway bridge across Steele Creek, a perfect place to take pictures if a logging train just happens to be passing by. If you turn right on the highway, then make an immediate right (don't go onto the railway bridge); you'll be on a disused spur road that quickly degenerates and becomes impassable. Not worth exploring, you might say—except that wildlife tends to use these older roads as thoroughfares, and it's not unusual to see a black bear galumphing along or disappearing into the underbrush.

III Woss Camp to Gold River

Not that long ago—until 1978—the road from Gold River to Woss Camp provided the only public land access to the north island. Those who travelled this route remember the gravel, the dust, the bonebreaking washboard at the end of a heavy logging season before the graders came through—and the fine scenery of lakes, rivers, and mountains. No one who had to travel this route more than once and who now uses the high-speed Highway 19 feels much nostalgia for the old days, but the logging-road route still exists, and is worth a look if you're not tired of gravel.

From the Woss Camp turn-off to the Gold River junction is about 80 kilometres along gravel roads that are generally good, though sometimes bumpy and rutted. The route is suitable for most drivers and vehicles; it is suitable only for those cyclists who like bone-rattling, teeth-jarring trips on gravel.

❧ ❧ ❧

Two starting points may be possible for this trip. The road that used to link the Zeballos Road to Woss along the south side of the Nimpkish River has been closed from time to time in recent years. A call to CanFor will clarify whether it's open—or, if you forgot to call, you can take the following short trip to check.

Optional: take the Zeballos Road west from Highway 19, cross the Nimpkish River a kilometre from the highway, and turn left 1.8 kilometres from the highway. A sign at this corner should indicate whether the road is closed. If the road is open, follow it some 24 kilometres along the bends and shallows of the Nimpkish River. The road emerges at Woss, where you can join the main route.

If the road is closed, or if you want a shorter back-road trip, **continue south on Highway 19 to the signposted turnoff to Woss. Turn right, and follow the road across the Nimpkish River bridge to a T-junction, about 1.2 kilometres from the highway. The road to the left goes to Gold River, but take a short side trip here by turning right and parking by the side of the road.** This is Woss Camp, with

Logging/tourist locomotive at Woss.

forest-company buildings and houses, a good display of logging paraphernalia, and a special feature. When it isn't taking tourists on the trip to Beaver Cove, steam logging locomotive 113 is parked here. The 113, a 135-ton Alco Rod Engine 2-8-2 built in the United States in 1920, came to Canada to work the Chemainus area in 1948, then to the north island in 1953. It worked regularly until 1966, and on special occasions until 1976. It was restored in 1988, and now steams along the tracks, pulling a forty-year-old Grey Ghost passenger car on tourist runs.

The 122-kilometre logging railway that CanFor uses in the Nimpkish Valley isn't just a tourist attraction: it's the longest working logging railway in North America. It started small, in 1917, with 10 kilometres of track and two steam engines, and has expanded to its present length, with four diesel engines, and 350 cars that carry timber from log-loading areas throughout the valley to the log sort at Beaver Cove. In an era where monster off-road and on-road logging trucks are the norm, the railway is well worth seeing. If you are a railway buff, you can obtain from CanFor a pamphlet that gives the history and technical details of the locomotives used on the tracks from 1918 to the 1960s.

Return to the junction and continue straight on along the Gold River road. This road is well signposted, usually for Gold River, occasionally for Vernon Lake. Half a kilometre from the junction, you will cross a bridge; just across the bridge, turn left for Vernon Lake. Straight on would take you to a campsite on the shore of Woss Lake, under the canopy of the forest, a pleasant place for camping, picnicking, and boating.

The road arrows past a swamp, then bears left 3.3 kilometres from the Woss Camp junction (signposted). Farther on, the Nimpkish River appears and disappears through a teenaged (in tree years) forest, with views of a snow-capped mountain in the distance.

About 20 kilometres from Woss Camp is an area containing the Nimpkish Island Ecological Reserve.

It's hard to travel in the north island without being torn by the conflicting claims of logging industry workers who fear for their jobs and the future of their families, and of those who plead that we must save more old-growth trees. If anything can tip the balance, this area of the Nimpkish Valley will.

"I came here in the early '70s," says a man who has seen the best and worst of the Vancouver Island forest. "This area was covered by a tremendous forest, older than the trees on Nimpkish Island. Those trees are

A loaded logging train on the Nimpkish Valley logging railroad.

maybe 360 years old; these trees were 670 years old. It was incredibly impressive."

All those oldest trees have been gone for more than twenty years. Unlike Carmanah, no battle was fought and won here to preserve an area of old growth large enough to survive. What is left is a small ecological reserve surrounded by the river. The current is eating away at the island, undermining the roots of the remaining old growth. The winds that roll down the valley, across the clear-cuts and young second growth, put added stress on the small grove of huge trees. Even visitors who want to marvel at the old trees unwittingly become one more stress that helps lead to their destruction.

Forty years ago, a logging company described the Nimpkish as "one of the outstanding timbered valleys on Vancouver Island." No one would so describe it these days.

Continue on to the left turn signposted for Vernon Lake, some 22 kilometres from Woss. If you're looking for a camp or picnic site, you can turn right here, to a large lakeside area, then continue on the Vernon Lake Road back to the main road. Otherwise, continue straight on, turning right on the signposted Gold River road another

2.8 kilometres along. The road straight ahead here leads to Klaklakama Lakes, a name that may derive from the native word meaning red surfaces, possibly a reference to iron ore in the vicinity.

All along the road now, you'll see signs warning operators of logging trucks and other equipment to keep their high-riding booms down, lest they snag power lines that carry 138,000 volts and run 12 or 13 metres above the road.

About 11.3 kilometres past the Vernon Lake turn, a road runs left to Vernon Camp. Though the camp isn't open to visitors, you can stop before you cross the bridge across the river, and peer up at the area where logs are loaded onto the logging railway cars.

Continue on the Gold River road. About 22 kilometres from the Vernon Lake turn-off, keep left; this road is signposted to Gold River, but the sign is definitely unobtrusive. A further 10 kilometres along, you leave CanFor forest lease land and enter Tree Farm Licence 19, Pacific Forest Products lease land, where logging traffic increases and danger signs multiply.

Sunset at Muchalat Lake, on the way to Gold River.

Some 38.6 kilometres from the Vernon lake turn-off, turn right to Muchalat Lake. A pleasant road curves down through old stumps and good-sized second growth to a camp and picnic site that is a favourite with Gold River residents for its location, view, picnic tables, and swimming float (really a boat and float plane dock, but a good place to catch late evening sun nonetheless).

Continue along the main Gold River road, through clear-cut and forest, with views of mountains where glaciers maintain a year-round icy presence. **You'll cross the Muchalat River, then 6 kilometres later, reach a long hill that slopes down to the river again.** Straight on at the bottom of the hill before the bridge is the 65-kilometre road to the mill town of Tahsis, on Tahsis Inlet. **Turn left, cross the river, and reach a junction. A right turn leads you to the instant mill town of Gold River,** built to serve the mill farther west at the inlet edge. The MV *Uchuck III* leaves from the end of Highway 28, serving Friendly Cove, Tahsis, and way points along the inlets that branch inland from the Pacific north of here.

Straight on leads you 90 kilometres on a paved and scenic highway across the island back to Campbell River and the end of the north island back-roads tours.

Maps

The following maps are for general reference only. Scales vary. Anyone who plans to drive any of the back-road routes, especially those that include logging roads, is strongly advised to acquire detailed maps of the territory they intend to cover. Recommended maps are listed with each tour.

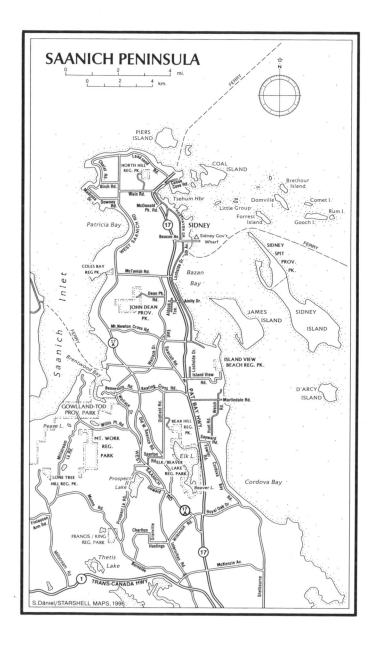

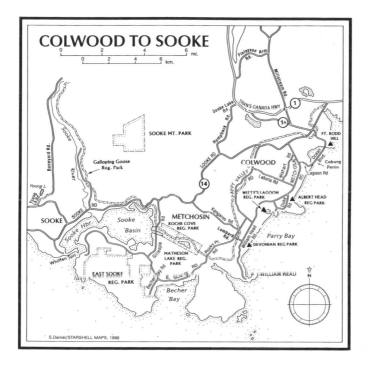

COLWOOD TO SOOKE

0   2   4   6 mi.

0   2   4   6 km.

SOOKE MT. PARK

Galloping Goose
Reg. Park

Boneyard Rd

Sooke River

Young L.

Sooke Lake Rd

Humpback Rd

TRANS-CANADA HWY

Finlayson Arm Rd

Millstream Rd

1

1A

FT. RODD
HILL

COLWOOD

SOOKE RD

14

Metchosin Rd

Lagoon Rd

Coburg
Penin

Latoria Rd

Happy Valley Rd

WITTY'S LAGOON
REG. PARK

ALBERT HEAD
REG PARK

SOOKE

Sooke Hbr.

Sooke Basin

METCHOSIN

ROCHE COVE
REG. PARK

Kangaroo Rd

Lombard Rd

Parry Bay

DEVONIAN REG PARK

William Head Rd

MATHESON
LAKE REG.
PARK

Whiffen Spit

Gillespie Rd

Rocky Pt Rd

WILLIAM HEAD

EAST SOOKE
REG. PARK

Becher
Bay

N

S.Daniel/STARSHELL MAPS, 1996

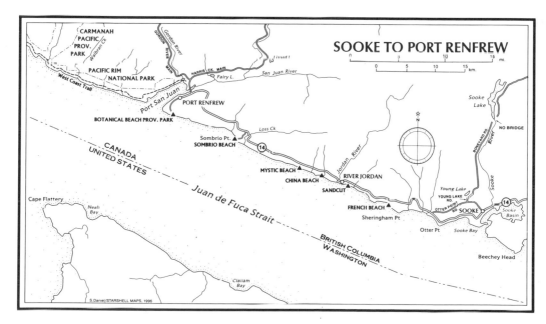

SOOKE TO PORT RENFREW

CARMANAH
PACIFIC
PROV.
PARK

PACIFIC RIM
NATIONAL PARK

West Coast Trail

Gordon River

GORDON RIVER MAIN

Malvan Ck

HARRIS CK. MAIN

Fairy L.

Lizard I.

San Juan River

0   5   10   15 mi.

0   5   10   15 km.

Sooke
Lake

Port San Juan

PORT RENFREW

BOTANICAL BEACH PROV. PARK

Loss Ck

Sombrio Pt.
SOMBRIO BEACH

14

Jordan River

N

NO BRIDGE

Boneyard Rd

Sooke River

CANADA
UNITED STATES

MYSTIC BEACH

CHINA BEACH

SANDCUT

RIVER JORDAN

Young Lake

YOUNG LAKE
RD

OTTER POINT
RD

SOOKE

14

Sooke
Basin

Cape Flattery

Neah
Bay

Juan de Fuca Strait

FRENCH BEACH

Sheringham Pt

Otter Pt

Sooke Bay

BRITISH COLUMBIA
WASHINGTON

Clallam
Bay

Beechey Head

S.Daniel/STARSHELL MAPS, 1996

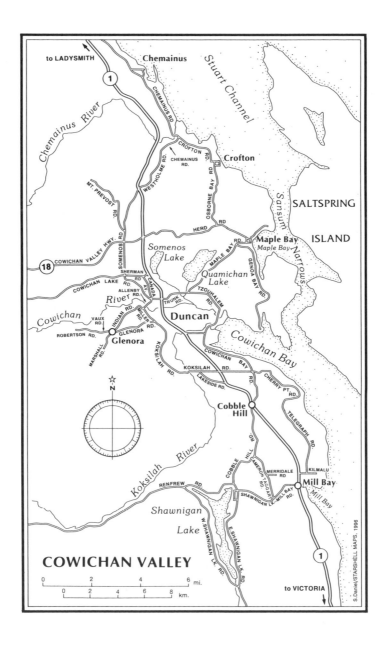

to LADYSMITH

Chemainus

Stuart Channel

1

Chemainus River

CHEMAINUS RD.

CROFTON

CHEMAINUS RD.

WESTHOLME RD.

Crofton

MT. PREVOST RD.

OSBORNE BAY RD.

SALTSPRING

HERD RD.

ISLAND

Sansum Narrows

SOMENOS RD.

COWICHAN VALLEY HWY.

18

COWICHAN LAKE RD.

Somenos Lake

MAPLE BAY RD.

Maple Bay
Maple Bay

SHERMAN RD.

CANADA AV.

Quamichan Lake

GENOA BAY RD.

ALLENBY RD.

TZOUHALEM RD.

River

TRUNK RD.

Duncan

Cowichan

VAUX RD.

INDIAN RD.

MILLER RD.

ROBERTSON RD.

MARSHALL RD.

GLENORA RD.

Glenora

Cowichan Bay

KOKSILAH RD.

COWICHAN BAY RD.

RD.

CHERRY PT. RD.

KOKSILAH RD.

LAKESIDE RD.

N

Cobble
Hill

TELEGRAPH RD.

Koksilah River

COBBLE HILL RD.

CAMERON-TAGGART RD.

MERRIDALE RD.

KILMALU

RENFREW RD.

SHAWNIGAN LK.–MILL BAY RD.

Mill Bay

Mill Bay

COWICHAN VALLEY

Shawnigan
Lake

W. SHAWNIGAN LK. RD.

E. SHAWNIGAN LK. RD.

1

to VICTORIA

0   2   4   6 mi.

0 2 4 6 8 km.

S. Daniel/STARSHELL MAPS, 1996

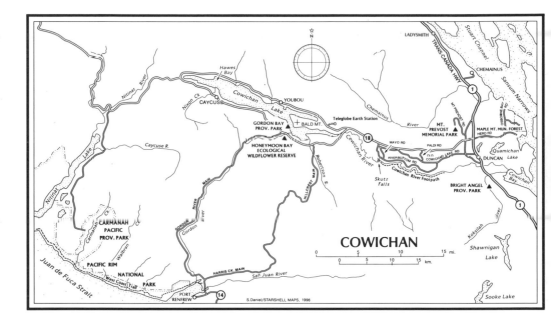

COWICHAN

S.Daniel/STARSHELL MAPS, 1996

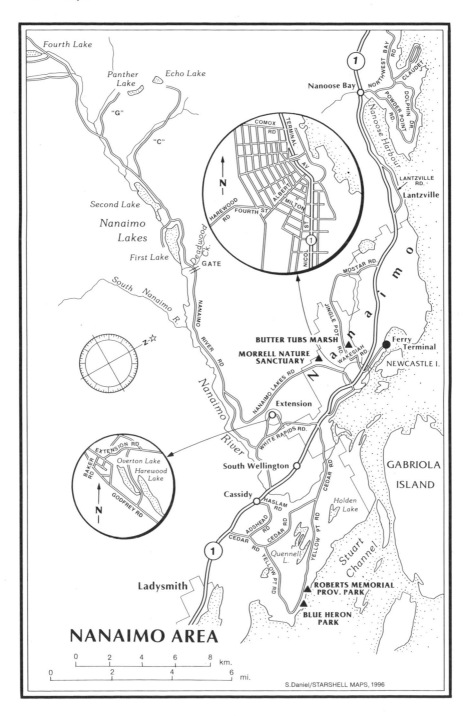

Fourth Lake

Panther Lake

Echo Lake

"G"

"C"

Second Lake

Nanaimo Lakes

First Lake

GATE

Deadwood Ck.

South Nanaimo R.

NANAIMO RIVER RD.

Nanaimo River

Nanaimo Lakes Rd.

COMOX RD.

TERMINAL AV.

HAREWOOD RD.

FOURTH ST.

ALBERT ST.

MILTON ST.

NICOL ST.

N

1

Nanoose Bay

1

NORTHWEST BAY RD.

CLAUDET RD.

DOLPHIN DR.

POWDER POINT RD.

Nanoose Harbour

LANTZVILLE RD.

Lantzville

MOSTAR RD.

JINGLE POT RD.

BUTTER TUBS MARSH

MORRELL NATURE SANCTUARY

WAKESIAH RD.

Ferry Terminal

NEWCASTLE I.

Nanaimo

Extension

WHITE RAPIDS RD.

CEDAR RD.

GABRIOLA

ISLAND

South Wellington

Holden Lake

Cassidy

HASLAM RD.

ADSHEAD RD.

CEDAR RD.

CEDAR RD.

YELLOW PT RD.

YELLOW PT RD.

Quennell L.

Stuart Channel

1

Ladysmith

ROBERTS MEMORIAL PROV. PARK

BLUE HERON PARK

EXTENSION RD.

BAKER RD.

Overton Lake

Harewood Lake

GODFREY RD.

N

N

NANAIMO AREA

0   2   4   6   8   km.

0   2   4   6   mi.

S.Daniel/STARSHELL MAPS, 1996

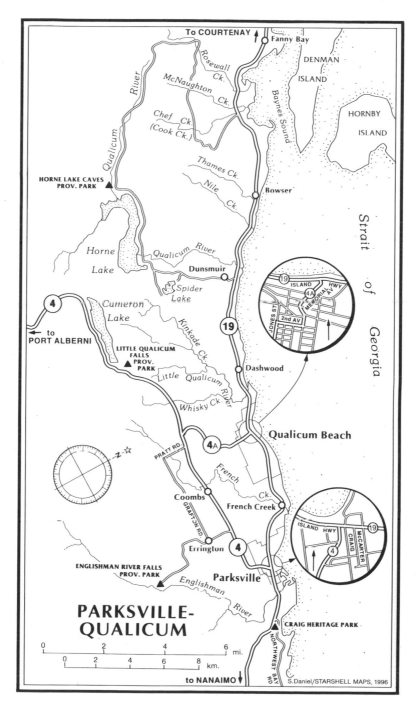

**PARKSVILLE-
QUALICUM**

To COURTENAY
Fanny Bay

DENMAN
ISLAND

Rosewall Ck.
McNaughton Ck.
Chef Ck.
(Cook Ck.)

Baynes Sound

HORNBY
ISLAND

Qualicum River

Thames Ck.
Nile Ck.

HORNE LAKE CAVES
PROV. PARK

Bowser

Qualicum River

Horne
Lake

Dunsmuir

Strait

Spider
Lake

Cameron
Lake

4

to
PORT ALBERNI

Kinkade Ck.

LITTLE QUALICUM
FALLS
PROV.
PARK

Little Qualicum River

Whisky Ck.

19

Dashwood

ISLAND HWY
19
4A
MEMORIAL AV
JONES ST.
2nd AV

of

Georgia

Qualicum Beach

4A

PRATT RD.

French

Ck.

Coombs

French Creek

GRAFTON RD.

ISLAND HWY
4
McCARTER
CRAIG
19

Errington

4

ENGLISHMAN RIVER FALLS
PROV. PARK

Englishman River

Parksville

CRAIG HERITAGE PARK

NORTHWEST BAY RD.

0   2   4   6 mi.
0   2   4   6   8 km.

to NANAIMO

S.Daniel/STARSHELL MAPS, 1996

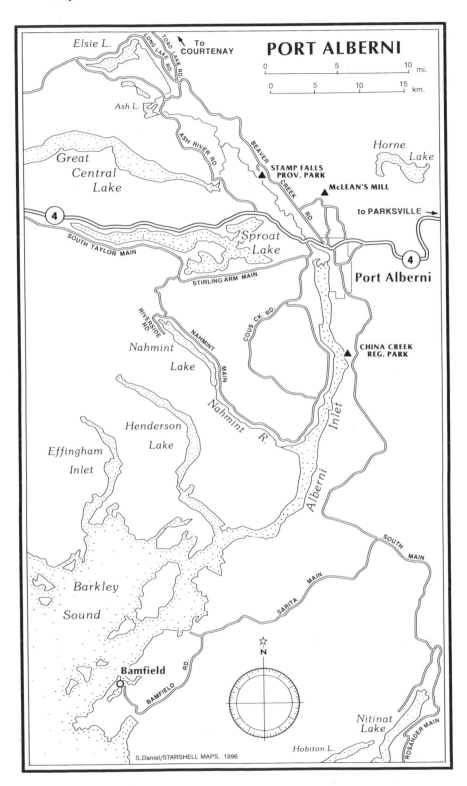

PORT ALBERNI

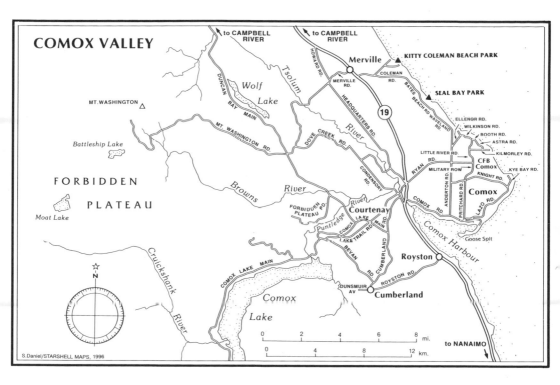

COMOX VALLEY

to CAMPBELL RIVER

to CAMPBELL RIVER

Merville

KITTY COLEMAN BEACH PARK

SEAL BAY PARK

Wolf Lake

MT. WASHINGTON △

Battleship Lake

F O R B I D D E N

P L A T E A U

Moat Lake

HEADQUARTERS RD.

MERVILLE RD.

COLEMAN RD.

BATES BEACH RD. WAVELAND RD.

ELLENOR RD.
WILKINSON RD.
BOOTH RD.
ASTRA RD.
KILMORLEY RD.

LITTLE RIVER RD.

CFB Comox

KYE BAY RD.

MILITARY ROW

KNIGHT RD.

RYAN RD.

ANDERTON RD.

PRITCHARD RD.

LAZO RD.

Comox

DUNCAN BAY MAIN

TSOLUM RIVER

HOWARD RD.

MT. WASHINGTON RD.

DOVE CREEK RD.

CONDENSORY RD.

Browns River

Puntledge River

FORBIDDEN PLATEAU RD.

Courtenay

COMOX LAKE MAIN

LAKE TRAIL RD.

BEVAN RD.

COMOX RD.

Comox Harbour

Goose Spit

Royston

Cruickshank River

N

Comox Lake

CUMBERLAND RD.

ROYSTON RD.

DUNSMUIR AV

Cumberland

0   2   4   6   8 mi.
0   4   8   12 km.

to NANAIMO

19

S. Daniel/STARSHELL MAPS, 1996

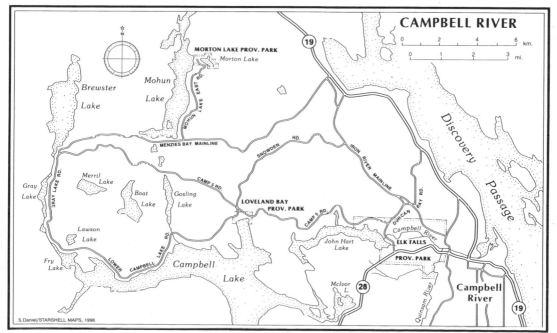

CAMPBELL RIVER

0   2   4   6 km.
0   1   2   3 mi.

N

MORTON LAKE PROV. PARK
Morton Lake

Brewster Lake

Mohun Lake

19

Discovery Passage

MENZIES BAY MAINLINE

MOHUN LAKE EAST RD.

SNOWDEN RD.

IRON RIVER MAINLINE

Gray Lake

Merril Lake

Boat Lake

Gosling Lake

3RAY LAKE RD.

CAMP 5 RD.

LOVELAND BAY PROV. PARK

Lawson Lake

John Hart Lake

Fry Lake

LOWER CAMPBELL LAKE RD.

CAMPBELL LAKE RD.

Campbell Lake

CAMP 5 RD.

DUNCAN BAY RD.

Campbell River

ELK FALLS PROV. PARK

Campbell River

McIvor L.

28

Quinsam River

19

S. Daniel/STARSHELL MAPS, 1996

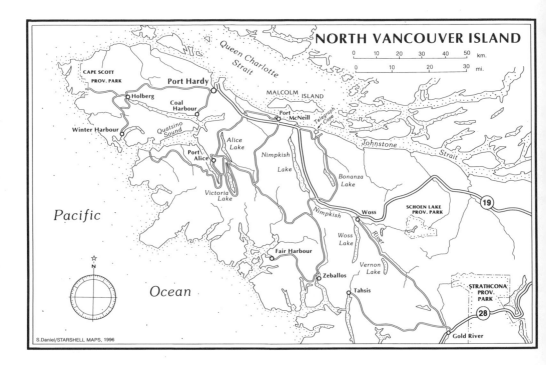

NORTH VANCOUVER ISLAND

| 0 | 10 | 20 | 30 | 40 | 50 | km. |

| 0 | 10 | 20 | 30 | mi. |

Queen Charlotte Strait

CAPE SCOTT
PROV. PARK

Port Hardy

Holberg

Coal Harbour

MALCOLM ISLAND

Port McNeill

Telegraph Cove

Winter Harbour

Quatsino Sound

Alice Lake

Port Alice

Nimpkish Lake

Johnstone Strait

Victoria Lake

Bonanza Lake

Pacific

Nimpkish

Woss

SCHOEN LAKE
PROV. PARK

19

Woss Lake

River

Fair Harbour

Vernon Lake

Zeballos

Tahsis

STRATHCONA
PROV.
PARK

Ocean

N

28

Gold River

S.Daniel/STARSHELL MAPS, 1996

Index

References to photographs are in *italics*.
Roads are listed under tour areas; tour names are in **bold** type.

About the Author

Rosemary Neering has been writing professionally for over twenty years. She is the author of many popular non-fiction books, including *Faces of British Columbia, In the Path of the Explorers, A Traveller's Guide to Historic British Columbia,* and the B.C. Book Prize winner *Down the Road: Journeys through Small-Town British Columbia.* She has also written a variety of educational books for children and teenagers, and has been a regular contributor to *Beautiful British Columbia* magazine. She lives in Victoria, B.C. When she leaves town, she always takes her time reaching her destination.